CONTENTS

About the Author

Bernard O'Connor has been a teacher for almost forty years and is the author of *Churchill's Angels, Churchill's Most Secret Airfield* and *Agent Rose*. He lives in Bedfordshire.

First published 2013

This edition first published 2014

Amberley Publishing
The Hill, Stroud
Gloucestershire, GL5 4EP

www.amberley-books.com

British Library Cataloguing in Publication Data.
A catalogue record for this book is available from the British Library.

ISBN 978 1 4456 4227 7 (paperback)
ISBN 978 1 4456 1178 5 (ebook)

Typeset in 10pt on 12pt Sabon.
Typesetting and Origination by Amberley Publishing.
Printed in the UK.

Foreword

I had never heard of Brickendonbury until I moved to Everton, a small village about halfway between Cambridge and Bedford. When I discovered that there was a Second World War airfield at the bottom of the hill (66 m) where I used to take my dog for walks, I asked about it in the Thornton Arms, the local pub. I was told that there was a gentleman in the village who had worked there during the war. Calling to see him, I asked if he could tell me anything about what went on at the airfield. He refused, arguing that he had signed the Official Secrets Act. Intrigued, I spent the next decade or so researching its history and publishing a number of books, the first being *RAF Tempsford: Churchill's Most Secret Airfield*. Two Special Duties squadrons were based there, flying off during the nights on either side of the full moon to drop tens of thousands of tons of supplies to resistance groups in countries across occupied Western Europe, parachuting over 2,000 agents and undertaking landing and pick-up operations in France.

Researching the stories of the women agents who were flown out, I necessarily found out about their training. Newspapers, magazines, biographies, autobiographies, memoirs, military histories, websites and recently released documents in the National Archives led me to publish *Churchill's Angels*.

Often being asked to give talks on the subject, I created a number of presentations, one of which was on the buildings requisitioned by the Special Operations Executive, a top-secret intelligence organisation during the war, where agents were trained in various aspects of clandestine warfare. I found evidence that over a thousand British and overseas personnel attended an industrial sabotage course at Brickendonbury Manor, near Hertford, about 20 miles north of London. Sparked by my commissioning editor to write another book, I undertook to research its history and the important role it played during the Second World War.

I need to acknowledge the work already done by Roderick Bailey, John Charrot, Freddie Clark, Igor Cornelissen, Bickham Sweet-Escott, Michael Foot, William Mackenzie, Sam McBride, Ray Mears, Russell Miller, Neil Rees, Jeffery Richelson, David Stafford, Des Turner, Ian Valentine and Hugh Verity, whose academic research has shed light on the events that follow. The National Archives' online catalogue allowed me to identify relevant documents and the staff there very kindly provided access to recently released correspondence and mission papers related to personnel in the Special Operations Executive. Kristina Lawson, Head of Market Information and Promotion at Brickendonbury, kindly provided photographs and details of the house's history. Rich Duckett helped locate George Rheam's notes on Brickendonbury. The Sandy and Potton library staff was very helpful in locating out-of-county books and articles from academic journals. Bonnie West, Senior Archive/ Library Assistant at Hertfordshire Archives and Local Studies, helped locate newspaper and journal articles. Hydro Vemork, Rjukan, kindly provided photographs of the heavy water plant; Mrs John Clarke of 'Nobby' Clarke; and Sam McBride of Frederick Peters. Steven Kippax needs special thanks. Not only was he able to locate and copy numerous personnel files, but he and members of the Special Operations Executive user group on yahoo.com have provided answers to my many queries and stimulated further research.

CHAPTER 1

Brickendonbury Manor's History until the Start of the Second World War, September 1939

Various books, journals and websites have detailed the history of the house and its gardens but few refer to its role during the Second World War. How long a house has stood on the site is unknown. While prehistoric people may have wandered through the nearby forested countryside, there is no evidence of an occupation site. Ermine Street, the Roman road from London to York, runs along the eastern boundary of the parish about half a mile away. During drainage work on the moat in 1893, 430 Roman coins, dated to about AD 250, were unearthed. Maybe they were hidden by someone worried about an attack, who then failed to return and recover them.

Hertford, an Anglo-Saxon settlement first recorded in 673, lies on the crossing point on the River Lea, about 2 miles to the north. Brickendon is also Anglo-Saxon, thought to mean Brica's hill. It would have been an advantageous site with a 72-metre promontory overlooking the wooded valley of Brickendon Brook to the south and west, the gently rising Hertford Heath to the east and a ridge and valley stretching down to the River Lea in the north.

Although the site is thought to have been occupied continuously since Saxon times, who owned the estate before 1016 is unknown. At that time it belonged to the canons of nearby Waltham Abbey, acknowledged by Edward the Confessor in 1061 and King Harold II shortly before the Norman Conquest. It is thought that, following the tradition of other landowners from northern France, a manor house was erected on the site and a moat constructed. The addition of the suffix -bury indicates a fortified site. A moat was constructed, not for defence, more as a source of fish for Fridays and throughout the forty days of Lent when everyone was expected not to eat meat.

King Henry II, following the murder of Thomas à Becket in 1170, granted the Liberty of Brickendon to the abbey as part of his penance. When Henry VIII broke with Rome, Waltham Abbey, like the monasteries, was dissolved; the estate was sold to Thomas Knighton in 1542. After Knighton sold it to Edmond Allen, in 1588 it was purchased by Stephen and his son William Soame or Soames for £1,000.

The present-day mansion dates back to about 1690 following Edward Clarke purchasing the estate in 1682 from the Soames family. Clarke was a Leicestershire merchant who, following the custom of those days, bought himself a large estate in pleasant countryside away from the noisy, dirty and overcrowded City of London. He moved to the capital after the Plague and Great Fire. Knighted in 1689, between 1690 and 1691 he was master of the Merchant Taylor's Company, and in 1696 Lord Mayor of London. He paid for a large, imposing mansion to be built on the site of the old manor house and, over successive generations, the house was extended and it was acquired through marriage by the Morgan family in the early eighteenth century. Charles Morgan was the Judge Advocate General and Judge Martial of Queen Anne's forces. Little did he know that his estate would be used for military training over 200 years later. His family were responsible for planting the avenue of trees, known as Morgan's Walk, which connects the mansion with Hertford.

In the late nineteenth century the estate was leased or let to a series of tenants, among them Russell Ellice, a director of the East India Company and its chairman in 1853. His ownership created the estate's first link with South East Asia.

The Morgans sold off plots of the estate in sales in 1873 and 1878 and in 1893 eventually sold the 1,000-acre estate to Charles Grey Hill, a Nottinghamshire lace merchant who died before he was able to move in. In 1893 George Pearson acquired the mansion and 1,054 acres, what was left of the estate, for £30,000. Both George and his son, Sir Edward Pearson, were associated with S. Pearson and Sons, major civil engineering contractors who were responsible for the construction of the Great Northern Railway and the City underground railway, which connected Hertford with Moorgate station in London.

On George Pearson's death in 1902, Sir Edward inherited the estate. A Justice of the Peace and high sheriff of Hertfordshire in 1909, he became Mayor of Hertford and was responsible for the construction of the town's war memorial. The Pearson family, which later established the media company Pearson plc, was responsible for much extension work, 'rebuilding the west end of the south front, adding an extra storey and, in 1919, a Jacobean-style banqueting hall, which now serves as the conference room ... The gardens were redeveloped to include, at the end of the moat, an artificial rock garden.'

Featured in the 1909 *Gardeners' Magazine*, Brickendonbury Manor was described as enjoying 'considerable fame for the extent, beauty, and high keeping of its gardens'.[1] There were photographs of Dutch gardens, rambling roses, a walled fruit border and a weeping ash tree overhanging the moat.

Following Sir Edward's death in 1925 his widow, Lady Pearson, moved out of the house and eventually rented the ivy-clad mansion to Stratton Park School. This was a private preparatory school for about fifty boys, which had relocated from Great Brickhill in Buckinghamshire. Their gymnasium with hooks in the ceiling for ropes is now the conference room and the swimming pool in the grounds is now a pond.

Towards the end of the 1930s, as a result of the economic depression, the number of students started to fall and, sometime before war broke out in 1939, Lady Pearson decided to sell the estate and the mansion. The school relocated to Benington House, at Hebing End near Stevenage, but the new owner, Ernest Gocher, a retired, unmarried butcher from Hoddesdon, was not able to move in. It was suggested that Lady Pearson mentioned the availability of the estate to the War Office.[2]

Fearful of the Luftwaffe bombing important government offices in London, the War Office was desperate for properties outside the city to house some of its departments. They duly requisitioned Brickendonbury, sometime in late 1939.[3]

CHAPTER 2

Brickendonbury and the Secret Intelligence Service, September 1939 – August 1940

Before the Second World War, the British Government relied on the Secret Intelligence Service (SIS), agents working undercover for the Foreign Office, and the War Office's Military Intelligence (MI) Directorate for information about what was going on in the rest of the world. However, with the rise of Adolf Hitler's Nazi party, the Sudeten Crisis and imminent prospect of Britain being at war, in March 1938 Lord Halifax (the newly appointed Foreign Secretary), Lord Hankey (Secretary to the War Cabinet) and Major Joe Holland of the Royal Engineers (and head of a military think tank) met with others in Whitehall and created an intelligence service which was independent from the SIS and MI. As the codename for the SIS was C, this new organisation was called Section D or Station IX. Holland was given a small 'research' section within Military Intelligence called MI[R], with a mandate to develop methods of irregular warfare.

Admiral 'Quex' Sinclair, then head of SIS, appointed forty-year-old Major Laurence Grand of the Royal Engineers to manage Section D. Grand had fought on the Indian Frontier and, on discovering that Pathans were raiding and stealing British ammunition, his idea was to place high explosive in every tenth round instead of the ordinary cordite. While some disapproved of this 'ungentlemanly' tactic,

Sinclair felt it was just the attitude Britain needed against potential enemies.

Michael Foot, the military historian, described Grand as being

> a striking personality, tall, handsome, well-tailored, with a heavy dark moustache; wore a red carnation; smoked cigarettes, almost without cease, through an elegant black holder; had an equally elegant wit. He was brim-full of ideas and energy, and he had a rare gift: he gave full trust to those under him and backed them up without question against outsiders. Unhappily he had a gift of rubbing staid men up the wrong way.[1]

The SIS headquarters in the basement of Broadway Buildings, 54 Broadway, opposite St James's Park underground station in London were too small to house Section D so Grand and his new staff moved round the corner into offices on the sixth floor of Caxton House, 2 Caxton Street. As more staff was needed, it took over the fifth floor as well. Part of the building included St Ermin's Hotel, where many SIS officers lunched and dined, entertained guests and interrogated potential recruits.

Unofficially, it was known as 'The Sabotage Service' and the D was said to stand for destruction. Its task was to come up with ideas for subversive operations in occupied Europe and develop ways of resourcing and implementing them. It was to include sabotage, labour unrest, go-slows, inflation and propaganda; anything that might weaken the enemy. In later years, Grand admitted it was like having to move pyramids with a pin.

Section D had four departments: Administration, Plans, Supplies and Execution. The Plans section, code name D/U, specialised in developing potential schemes and operations. The Supplies section was divided into propaganda, communications, personnel and technical. Within the technical research sections were D/D and D/X. D/D dealt with 'research and development of an engineering nature, small mechanisms and devices, including firearms'. D/X was the Laboratory section, which dealt mainly with explosives, incendiary devices and detonators. The

Execution section was not filled with assassins; it was responsible for liaising with the Royal Navy, the Royal Air Force and the Army to ensure that the planned operations received any necessary help in transport and logistics.

It needs to be remembered that the SIS was a 'hush-hush' organisation and its entire staff had to sign the Official Secrets Act. Known today as MI6, it neither confirms nor denies its involvement in any overt (open) or covert (hidden) operations. After the war, Lieutenant-Commander Arthur Langley, an SIS officer, admitted that the conditions of employment were simple:

> One was not officially employed by anybody. One was paid in cash; there was no security, no pension or health plan. One did not render any income tax return. Officially one had failed to exist. An assignment would be given to fulfil as best one could, usually outside the law; if one was caught either by the police of one's own country or the counter-intelligence organisation of another, one would be officially disowned.[2]

A subsection of the Personnel section was responsible for training and it was Kim Philby, recruited from his job as correspondent for *The Times*, who shed light on the origins of Brickendonbury as a training school for spies. In his book, *My Silent War: The Autobiography of a Spy*, he recalled going into the office on Caxton Street and being surprised to meet Guy Burgess, an old friend from his days at Trinity College, Cambridge. Section D's aims, he was told, were to help defeat the enemy by stirring up active resistance in occupied countries and destroying their sources of power by non-military means. Burgess told him that in July 1939 he had proposed to Grand that they establish a school for training agents in the techniques of underground work.

> It was an astonishing proposal, not because it was made, but because it had not been made before. No such school exisited. Guy argued the case for its necessity, obvious now but new then. He outlined the

subjects of a syllabus. At the end, he suggested that such a college should be named the 'Guy Fawkes College' to commemorate an unsuccessful conspirator 'who had been foiled by the vigilance of the Elizabethan SIS.' It was a neat touch. He could hardly have proposed 'Guy Burgess College.'[3]

A less obvious title was chosen – 'The Inter-Service Experimental Department' – but to those in the know, it was called 'D School'. According to the SIS website, Burgess's syllabus at Brickendonbury included propaganda, organisation of subversive cells, the art of spreading rumour and propaganda, the use of arms and explosives, wireless telegraphy, etc.[4] Burgess had been recruited into Section D in January 1939 from the BBC's talks department and, with Philby's awareness of irregular warfare from his experiences of reporting for *The Times* on the Spanish Civil War, he was assigned the task of devising the school's training course.

At last, I had got my teeth into something. I broke the subject up into its component parts: syllabus, selection of trainees, security, accommodation and so on, and produced a memorandum on each. I have forgotten most of what I wrote and in view of the huge training establishment that gradually developed. I hope that my first modest paper on the subject no longer exists, having deposited his shower of sparks into my lap, Guy seemed to lose interest in a fresh riot of ideas. But it was not so. He saw that Grand read my papers, and arranged committees to discuss them. I did not take to committee work then, and have never taken to it since. Every committee has its bugbear. My bugbear on the training committee was a certain Colonel Chidson. He had played an astute part in rescuing a lot of industrial diamonds from Hitler in Poland, but to me he was a pain in the neck. He had visions of anarchy stalking Europe, and resisted bitterly the whole idea of letting a lot of thugs loose on the Continent. One day, I spotted him coming towards me in Lower Regent Street. A moment later, he saw me and froze in his tracks. In a swift recovery, he turned up his coat collar and dived into a side-street. Our training school became very necessary.

Guy's refrain at the time was 'the idea must be made to catch on', and somehow it did. In due course, I learnt to my surprise that Brickendonbury Hall, a former school building in spacious grounds near Hertford, had been acquired for training purposes. I was introduced to a Commander Peters, RN, who had been seconded to us to act as a commandant of the school. He often took Guy and me to dinner at the Hungaria, to listen to our views on the new project. He had faraway naval eyes and a gentle smile of great charm. Against all the odds, he took a great and immediate fancy to Guy, who ruthlessly swiped the cigarettes off his desk. He was the type of strong sentimentalist … Our trainees came to adore him.[5]

Forty-year-old Frederick Peters joined the Royal Navy during the First World War and was the first Canadian to be awarded the Distinguished Service Order. Most of the interwar years he worked on the Gold Coast, what is now Ghana, manufacturing specialised pumps for midget submarines. He rejoined the Navy in 1939 and commanded a flotilla of anti-submarine trawlers, earning the Distinguished Service Cross. To then be given a desk job administering a sabotage school must have been a change after life at sea.

There were three short pamphlets available that would have been of particular interest to Grand and his colleagues. *The Art of Guerrilla Warfare* and *The Partisan Leader's Handbook – A Tactical Guide* were written by Major Colin Gubbins in the spring of 1939 as practical guides to sabotage. Recruited to Section D by Major Holland, he had made an intensive study of the Irish Republican Army's and the Communists' doctrine and methods of guerrilla warfare and was responsible for setting up the first Special Forces training school at Inverailort, a remote estate in Inverness-shire. According to Jenkins, Gubbins's basic principles were

surprise, swift and sudden attacks then immediate withdrawal; never hold ground, always plan the line of retreat; mobility; be sure of exact intelligence and clear knowledge about the ground where they will operate – usually near their own home – so that they already knew every path, lane, every hollow; if it is far from home then only use reliable guides.

The third, *How to Use High Explosives*, was written by Major Millis Jefferis, a Royal Engineer. According to Jenkins, it included simple tips on

> how a saboteur could attack, with ease and profit, motor car or lorry or bus axles, railway engine pistons, tramline or railway points, telephone junction boxes, electricity substations ... if you wanted to ruin a whole shed full of engines, always cripple the same part of each one otherwise the one could be mended by cannibalising another. He details which kind of bridges are or are not readily breakable with small charges, where these charges had to be placed, how their size was to be worked out, how they were to be laid, tamped, hidden if need be and fired ... the advantages of a stout hammer – in those days many machines rested on cast-iron bases, which would crack if hit hard, thus rendering the machine unsafe to use.

These pamphlets were translated into many languages and distributed to agents attending the training courses at Brickendonbury. *The Partisan Leader's Handbook* contained the principles of guerrilla warfare and sabotage; road ambush; rail ambush; the destruction of an enemy post, detachment or guard; concealment and care of arms and explosives; the enemy's information system and how to counter it; how to counter enemy action; guerrilla information service and sabotage methods. The last section provided the current definition of sabotage and listed the targets:

> Sabotage means any act done by individuals that interferes with the enemy and so helps your people to defeat him. It covers anything from the shooting of a sentry to the blowing up of an ammunition dump. The following are various acts, and the best way of carrying out the difficult ones: -

1 Lorries, cars, tanks, etc.: - Burn them by knocking a hole in the bottom of the petrol tanks, and setting fire to the escaping petrol.

If you can't burn them, put water or sugar in the petrol tanks, or remove the magneto, etc. This will temporarily disable the vehicle.

2 Munition Dumps: - The best method is to lay a charge of explosives among the shells, and then explode it, but it will be rare that you will get an opportunity to do this unless you are disguised as an enemy soldier. There are other ways. If the dump is in a building, a good way is to set fire to the building. Use oil-soaked rags, shavings, thermite bomb.

If the dump is in an open field or by the road, throw a special bomb into it (this must be a bomb with at least one kilogramme of explosive in it, and you must hit a shell or it will not be effective).

3 Cement: - Open the sacks, and pour water on them, or leave them for rain and moisture to get in.

4 Hay, forage: - Burn or throw acid or disinfectant.

5 Petrol stocks: - Use a special bomb or thermite bomb.

6 Refrigerator shed, and refrigerator railway vans: - Destroy the refrigerating apparatus.

7 Sniping and killing sentries, stragglers, etc: - Get a rifle or revolver, but use a knife or noose when you can. This has a great frightening effect. Don't act unless you are certain you can get away safely. Night-time is best and has the best effect on enemy nerves. Get used to moving about in the dark yourself. Wear rubber shoes and darken your face.

8 Telegraph lines on roads and railways: - Cut these whenever possible. When you cannot reach them, throw a rope with a weight on the end and try and drag them down. Cut down a tree so that it will fall across them.

9 Railways: - Jam the points by hammering a wooden wedge into them. Cut signal wires.

Set fire to any coaches and wagons you can get at. If you can use explosive, try and destroy the points. Remember that railways can carry very little traffic if the signalling apparatus is interfered with, and this traffic must go very slowly.

10 Water Supplies: - Contaminate water which is used by the enemy. Use paraffin, strong disinfectants, salt etc.

11 Destruction of leading marks, buoys, lightships, etc. in navigable waters.

12 Burning of soldiers' cinemas, theatres: - Cinema films are highly inflammable [*sic*]. The cinema should be fired during a performance by firing of the films in the operator's box. This should be easily arranged.

13 Time bombs, cigar shaped, are very suitable for placing in trains, lorries, etc. They are made of lead tubing, divided into two halves by a copper disc. Suitable acids are put in each half, and when they have eaten the acid away, the acids combine and form an intensely hot flame, which will set fire to anything with which it comes into contact. The thickness of the copper disc determines when the bomb will go off. Get some of these bombs.[6]

One of Grand's initial ideas was to establish 'stay behind' sabotage parties in those countries threatened by German invasion who could destroy vital economic and military targets. One imagines that Peters was able to recommend potential targets in harbours and dock facilities and identify exactly which were the best places on a ship to place explosives to ensure it sank.

Grand appointed Burgess as second in command in the hope that his ideas would come to fruition. Philby considered that Burgess's experiences working for the BBC and MI5 amply endowed him with the qualities needed for running what became called the 'D School'. However, experts in sabotage were needed.

One of the first people that Grand appointed was forty-six-year-old George Hill, who had worked for the SIS in Russia during the First World War. During the Russian Revolution, he won the Military Cross for his work helping the anti-Bolshevik White Army. On his return to England, Hill contacted his literary agent who commissioned him to write three articles on his sabotage operations for a new magazine, *The*

War, at thirty guineas each. The first covered the basics of sabotage, the unarmed combat weapon of a civilian population under enemy occupation. It included the dropping of lumps of sugar in a petrol tank, putting a handful of fine sand in the hot box of a railway truck, using a sharp knife to puncture a tyre, cutting telegraph wires and the changing of destination labels on railway trucks to cause confusion on congested railway, tricks that he had practised in Russia and occupied Ukraine in 1917 and 1918.

The article must have been read by Major Grand, who, after entertaining Hill for lunch on the fourth floor of St Ermin's Hotel, invited him to join D Section. On accepting the job, he was allocated Northern Europe as his 'parish', so he began by collecting intelligence on each country, the leading personalities in politics, the press, the Russian intelligence service, French diplomatic and consular representatives, the strength of the police and the German influence and menace.

Needing to update his knowledge of high explosives, he attended an explosives course at Aston House outside Stevenage and, after training in codes and cyphers, went to France to liaise with members of the Deuxième Bureau de l'Etat Major General, France's military intelligence, whom he had known in Paris before the war. When his attempt to supply the Belgian Resistance with explosives and detonators, what he called sweets and toys, was thwarted by the German advance, he drove a modified Rolls-Royce to Bordeaux and caught the last cruiser back to England in June 1940. He was then sent by Grand to help run his newly established industrial sabotage school at Brickendonbury with oversight of the training of the agents destined to be parachuted into Occupied Europe. While at Brickendonbury, with D's agreement, Hill set up a separate skeleton section to deal with developments in the USSR.[7]

The Army's standard method of blowing up buildings was placing large quantities of guncotton inside and setting it alight. Guncotton or 'collodion' cotton was nitrocellulose, the same chemical used to make ping-pong balls, guitar picks, nail polish and wood varnish. It was made by adding nitric acid to carded cotton, flax or other shredded woody fibre. Although highly flammable and light to carry, large quantities were needed, which would be highly visible to workers or guards at the target. This made it unsuitable for the sort of sabotage operations planned by Section D. Instead they needed explosives that were light to carry, could be concealed easily and needed only small quantities to do the destructive work.

Dynamite, invented in 1867 by Alfred Nobel, the Swedish chemist of Peace Prize fame, was being widely used in mining and quarrying operations. It was made by mixing nitroglycerine with powdered kieselguhr, a type of soil, or other absorbent material like powdered shells, clay, sawdust or wood pulp, rolling it into sticks and covering it with protective coating. Nobel had discovered that mixing liquid nitroglycerine with silica made it malleable. In order for it to explode, he used a blasting cap that he had invented in 1863. Rather than using heat combustion, the strong shock caused the dynamite to explode. However, as the nitroglycerine would often leak through its packaging, it was highly unstable for potential saboteurs to carry in their haversacks. Also, the blasting cap needed a long fuse, which would be easily spotted with observant eyes.

The first solution was gelignite, also known as blasting gelatin or jelly, which Nobel invented in 1875. This was nitrocellulose dissolved in either nitroglycerine or nitroglycol and then mixed with wood pulp and saltpetre (potassium nitrate or sodium nitrate). Unlike dynamite, it did not 'sweat' so it was safe to handle without protection. It was also malleable and could be cut into whatever sized pieces were necessary.

The second solution was the time pencil. This was based on a model Gubbins brought back from Poland in 1938, and was perfected by Arthur Langley at Aston House. He stressed that at the heart of nearly all sabotage operations was a time fuse – one that could be set to go off in minutes or weeks.

It must preferably be very small, easy to operate, easy to make, silent (no clicking from a clock), immune to vibration or bumping about, unaffected by changes in ambient temperature (to function equally well in the Arctic or the Tropics), have a good shelf life, be safe to handle and finally, be constructed of common easily available materials in wide supply with no identification marks on them, so that if found by an enemy he would not be able to prove where it was manufactured.[8]

The time pencil was the SOE's preferred method for operations in 'The Field', their euphemism for Occupied Europe. Large-scale diagrams that explained how it worked were handed around. It was about the size of a fountain pen and had three parts. A thin copper tube at one end contained a glass ampoule of copper chloride. The detonator was in the middle. When the copper end was pressed hard, the glass broke. This released the acid which started to corrode a steel wire. When it snapped, it released a spring-loaded striker which fired a percussion cap that ignited the plastic explosive, what the French called *plastique*. What determined the time you had to get away safely before it blew up was the concentration of acid.

A coloured strip was stuck on the side of the pencil. Black meant, in theory, that they had ten minutes' delay, red thirty minutes', green six hours', yellow, twelve and blue, twenty-four. They had to make sure the glass broke though.

Hill described Philby as being quick, perceptive and full of ideas and sound advice. He mentioned that Burgess got into trouble within the first few weeks when a corporal complained that he had been 'trying to muck about with him'. This did not lead to his dismissal, just transfer to another unit.[9] Philby described Hill as 'jolly' George, 'one of the few living Englishmen who had actually put sand in axle-boxes. Immensely paunchy, he looked rather like Soglow's king with a bald pate instead of a crown.'[10] One imagines Hill gave the students the benefit of his experiences in industrial sabotage. Deacon described him as living up to his previous reputation as a first-class intelligence man and an exceptional agent.[11]

Philby identified some of the other members of staff at Brickendonbury. There was an unnamed melancholy Czech printer whom Grand had recommended, as he had run an underground press in Prague. He was 'pale and podgy and after one look at him the Commander decided that he had to eat in the mess with the students'.[12] One imagines that he gave information to the students about the various clandestine ways of producing and disseminating propaganda.

There was also a 'Mr Werner', described as a 'sad' Austrian Social-Democrat who was being trained to lead any potential Austrian students. Philby said he resigned when none arrived for lessons; he was posted to Egypt but the submarine that took him was sunk by dive-bombers in the Mediterranean.

The man given charge of the running of the house was Spanish-speaking Tomás 'Tommy' Harris, a remarkable painter and art dealer and one of Burgess's friends from before the war. Philby described him as 'a glorified house-keeper', largely because he and his wife, Hilda, were inspired cooks and had a reputation for throwing lavish house parties. 'The work was altogether unworthy of his untaught but brilliantly intuitive mind.'[13] Their friendship, he admitted, was the only bright part of his stay at Brickendonbury and, of all the staff, Harris was the only one who acquired, in those first few weeks, any sort of personal contact with the students.

A few trainees were tossed our way: two small groups of Belgians and Norwegians, and a somewhat larger group of Spaniards. In all, there were about twenty-five of them. Perhaps they picked up some useful tips at Brickendonbury, but I doubt it. We had no idea what tasks they were supposed to perform and Guy and I had no success in digging the necessary information out of London headquarters. Otherwise, we had little to do except talk to the Commander and help him draft memoranda for headquarters which seldom vouchsafed a reply. One thing was clear. We had little to teach the Spaniards, most of whom were *ex-dinamitros* from Asturias. 'All instructors are the same,' remarked one – a boy of about eighteen. 'They tell you to cut off so much fuse. We double it to be quite safe. That is why we are still alive.'[14]

Security at Brickendonbury during the time the SIS were there was not as good as it ought to have been. Burgess had decided that, as their students were likely to be sent into enemy territory, he did not want them divulging their instructors' real names should they be captured and interrogated. Philby reported that Peters's alias was Thornley and Hill was Dale, but he would not reveal the name he had been given. Only Harris was known as Harris and it was he who reported after the war that he had met the head of the Belgian group at Brickendonbury, 'a nasty man of carefully obtruded aristocratic origin'. Apparently, one of the students had penetrated all their aliases except Philby's. As Burgess was code-named DU, he gave Philby the code name DUD.[15]

Philby reported an amusing incident before Burgess was 'transferred' to take up other work:

Night had just fallen after a fine summer day. The Commandant was in bed, nursing a sharp attack of eczema, to hide which he was growing a beard. A visiting instructor under the name of Hazlitt, was at his bedside sipping a glass of port. There was a sudden shout from the garden, which was taken up by a Babel in five langauges. Trainees poured into the house, claiming to have seen, one, three, ten, any number of parachutes falling in the vicinity. On hearing the news, the Commander ordered the Belgians to get into uniform and mount a machine-gun in the French-windows. It commanded a nice field of fire, right across the school playing grounds. I do not know what would have happened if the enemy had come in by front door. 'If the Germans had invaded,' the Commander told Hazlitt, 'I shall get up.'

He then made a disastrous mistake. He instructed Guy to ascertain the exact facts of the case, and telephone the result to the duty officer in London. Guy went about the business with a wicked conscientiousness. I heard snatches of his subsequent telephone report. 'No, I cannot add to what I have said ... You wouldn't want me to falsify evidence, would you? Shall I repeat? ... Parachutes have been seen dropping in the neighbourhood of Hertford in numbers varying from eighty to none ... No I cannot differentiate between the credibility of the various witnesses. Eighty to none. Have you got that? I will call you again if necessary. Goodbye.' He went to report in triumph. 'I don't know what I shall do if I do get up,' said the Commander, 'but I shall certainly take command.'

An hour or two passed, and nothing happened. The Belgians sadly took apart their Lewis gun, and we all went to bed. Next morning, Guy spent a lot of time on the telephone, and periodically spread gleeful tidings. The Duty Officer had alerted his Chief, who had communicated with the War Office. Eastern Command had been pulled out of bed, its armour grinding to action stations in the small hours. Guy made several happy guesses at the cost of the operation, upping it by leaps and bounds throughout the day. I should add that the nil estimate given him the night before was my own; the eighty, I should think, came from Guy himself. Both of us were wrong. One parachute had fallen. Attached to a land-mine, it had draped itself harmlessly round a tree.[16]

During the 'Phoney War', September 1939 until Germany invaded Holland, Belgium and France in May 1940, British government propaganda made people fearful of heavy bombing raids and an impending invasion. This worry was intensified with the evacuation from Dunkirk of over 300,000 Allied troops between the end of May and the beginning of June. Some in the War Office realised that the only way Britain could win the war was by invading France and pushing the Germans back. To do so successfully, Britain needed the support of those people who opposed the German occupation of their country and were prepared to do something about it.

Hugh Dalton, the Minister for Economic Warfare, campaigned with Lord Halifax, Lord Hankey and Colonel Holland, the men who created D Section, concerned that the organisation was too dependent on SIS and MI5. They met with senior officials in the Foreign Office, the War Office and the SIS, arguing that the best way to defeat the Germans was to combine conventional military methods with a 'war from within'. Dalton suggested that a new organisation could 'coordinate, inspire, control and assist opposition groups, resistance movements and nationalist uprisings'.

Dalton considered Section D to be too small and ineffectual. Instead of a 'Robin Hood' approach with contracts for supplies not going through official channels, he wanted the organisation run more efficiently, with forms filled out and products 'passed' by official inspectors. Kim Philby noted that Grand never had the financial resources to implement his ideas. They tended to be given only a lukewarm reception by the Armed Forces, and the Treasury blocked his requests. His imagination and enthusiasm were not matched by his management ability. Dalton wanted an intelligence service that was less dependent on the Foreign Office and the War Office and funded directly by the government.

They went to see Winston Churchill, who had just been appointed Prime Minister and First Lord of the Admiralty, with a plan to set up an independent intelligence agency. Churchill was said to have loved the idea and asked Neville Chamberlain, who had just resigned as Prime Minister, to draft its charter. On 22 July 1940, after several revisions, the Cabinet signed the charter creating the Special Operations Executive (SOE). It amalgamated Section D, MI(R) and Electra House, the Foreign Office's secret propaganda unit.[17]

Its function was to promote sabotage against the enemy by encouraging subversive activities, spreading political discontent and disrupting their means of transport and communication. In order to achieve these aims they needed to support the various resistance groups by dropping arms, equipment and agents and lifting their important leaders out and bringing them to safety back in Britain.

Peters grew increasingly taciturn and withdrawn over the summer of 1940. Word spread that Section D was going to be absorbed within the newly formed organisation under the control of Dr Dalton, the Minister of Economic Warfare. Grand's place was taken by Sir Frank Nelson, described by Philby as 'a humourless businessman'. This was shortly followed by a visit to Brickendonbury by Major Colin Gubbins, recruited to Section D by Major Holland. He arrived at Brickendonbury with a posse of fresh-faced officers, who barked at each other and at us, the Commander fell into a deep depression. He minded not being told. It was no surprise when he summoned Guy and myself one morning and told us that he had spent the previous evening composing his letter of resignation. He spoke sadly, as if conscious of failure and neglect. Then he cheered up and the charming smile came back, for the first time in many days. He was clearly happy to be going back to his little ships after his brief baptism of political fire.[18]

The students were sent away, with the SIS staff disbanded. Harris, described as a natural intelligence officer, proved his worth over the six months, with his wife's help, feeding everyone at Brickendonbury. He was transferred to work with MI5 in their Iberian section.[19] According to Philby, he was to conceive and guide one of the most creative intelligence operations of all time. Burgess and Philby were transferred to Gubbins's office at 64 Baker Street where, when Philby opened his monthly pay packet from the SOE, he found ten five-pound notes. After what he called 'the abortive Brickendonbury experiment', he was transferred to Beaulieu, SOE's 'Finishing School' in the New Forest, where he delivered a course in propaganda.[20]

Following the German invasion of Russia in June 1942, Hill was appointed to head the SOE's mission in Moscow and was involved in arranging the sending of thirty-four Soviet agents to Britain to be infiltrated into German-occupied territory. As their missions did not include industrial sabotage, they were not sent on any of the training courses.

It was mentioned earlier that Hill had attended a course at Aston House, an ivy-covered mansion near Stevenage. This was another of the requisitioned properties used by Section D, set in 5 acres of parkland about 30 miles north of London. It was a short drive from Knebworth railway station and the Great North Road and only 10 miles northwest of Brickendonbury. It was known initially as E.S.6. (WD) and later as Station XII. On 25 August 1939, Major Holland set up a small 'research' section called MI(R) whose personnel were allocated the task of identifying suitable military and economic targets, developing ideas on irregular ways of sabotaging them as well as collecting useful military, political and economic information. It was termed by some as the 'Statistical Research Department of the War Office', shortened to the 'Statistical Research Centre', 'SRC' or 'SRD'. This section was initially based at Bletchley Park, another requisitioned country house, near Newport Pagnell in Buckinghamshire, about 50 miles north-west of London. They were not there for long as the property was allocated to the Government's Code and Cypher School, which became known as Station X. In November 1939, they were transferred to Aston House.

Holland recruited Major Millis Jefferis, who had just returned from a sabotage and intelligence-gathering mission in Norway, and Colonel Stuart Macrae, an engineer who had worked on cluster bombs during the First World War and who was editor of *Armchair Science*. They were given the task of researching and developing limpet bombs and other explosive devices.

On 9 January 1940, Aston House became ISRB XII, ostensibly the Radio Communications Department. ISRB was the Inter Services Research Bureau, the cover name for the SOE, said to allow the members of the Army, Navy and Air Force to enter the HQ on Baker Street without raising too many questions. Under the cover name of Signals Development Branch Depot No. 4, War Office, it was used initially for wireless research but then taken over by Langley for research and development into weapons and explosives.

In Des Turner's account of Aston House, he interviewed Langley, its first Commanding Officer, whom he credits with the invention of the time pencil fuse as well as being the first person to purloin and experiment with plastic explosive as a sabotage weapon. With the help of a professor of chemistry from the University of London, Langley 'evolved a little time fuse about the size of a pencil. It could set off incendiary bombs or high explosives. For its time delay it depended upon a corrosive solution eating through a fine steel wire.' Its action was simple; when the agent pressed a ridge on the pencil, acid was released, which ate through a wire attached to a detonator at a rate that could be carefully preset, thus allowing the agent to reach cover; it would prove so reliable that, by the end of the war, 12 million had been produced. The pencil fuse was also cheap, Langley chirruped: 'All you needed, except for a little ampoule of corrosive liquid, could be bought at the local ironmongers or hardware store. Any chemist capable of doing a little glass-blowing could produce the ampoule.'[21]

Langley recalled having to study the acts of sabotage committed by German agents during the First World War. Incendiary bombs with time-delay fuses had been concealed in ships in foreign ports whose cargoes were destined for Britain. Set to go off when the ship left port, it was hoped that they would sink and block the harbour. Trying to find out what the enemy was doing twenty years earlier, imagining what new developments they had up their sleeve and planning effective countermeasures were all part of his job. At a large chalk quarry in the grounds of Aston House, he and his staff experimented with various explosives, eventually working out exactly how much was needed to blow a hole in the hull of a ship to ensure it sank, to blow up or derail a steam train or an electric locomotive, to shatter a tank's metal tracks, destroy an electricity substation, bring down a pylon, blow a hole in a water pipe or even open a locked safe.

Colonel Leslie Wood, Langley's replacement as Commanding Officer at Aston House, noted that,

> We invented, made, supplied and trained personnel in the use of 'toys', not only for the resistance but for all the special forces: Commandos, Small Boat Section, Airborne Division and Long Range Desert Patrol … We had magazines for explosives and sheds in which to handle them and large storehouses for incendiaries and all the rest of our 'toys', and workshops wherein to experiment and manufacture. We designed and made up special explosive charges tailored for the job in hand and simple to place and fire by any commando or resistance worker.[22]

One can see that Aston House and Brickendonbury had a close relationship so that those students destined for sabotage missions would attend courses at both houses. Security was tighter at Aston, where, although they used cover names, the staff wore civilian clothes and sunglasses during the summer. Only those who needed to be there were allowed into the main house and workshops. The saboteurs were taken to the quarry, practised with the explosives and then left. Aston's job was to research and produce the 'toys'; Brickendonbury's job was to train volunteers to go into the field, 'play' with the toys and then run away.

CHAPTER 3

Brickendonbury and the Special Operations Executive, August 1940 – June 1945

When the SOE took over the running of Brickendonbury and started their training classes in August 1940, the syllabus remained largely unchanged. Until he was transferred to Beaulieu, Philby taught basic espionage tradecraft and Langley instructed students at Aston House on how to derail trains by using only a plum-sized lump of plastic explosive.

There were discussions about whether the estate should be 'open' with security personnel frequenting the local area keeping their eyes and ears open for potential security risks or whether it should be 'closed' with dog patrols and armed guards. The 'open' system was decided upon, but guards on the entry would not allow access to unauthorised personnel. Passes were issued to those in the know.

As small quantities of plastic explosives can produce a great deal of destuction, a specially built explosives store was constructed some distance from the main house. A contingent of FANYs, young women from the First Aid Nursing Yeomanry, was drafted in to undertake the domestic arrangements, the cooking, and the laundry, administrative and driving duties. Sue Ryder, who later set up Sue Ryder homes, was stationed temporarily at Brickendonbury. She reported that the only breach in security occurred when a group of boys from the nearby

Haileybury school trespassed and were caught swarming around the aeroplane and tank park. No doubt the headmaster had very stern words with them.

> Though our days were full and passed quickly a few of the students and FANYs at the school sometimes had an overwhelming urge to go out for a while. This was not permitted, but all the same we would, very occasionally, go out from Station 17 for a swift ride in the surrounding country on the light collapsible bikes [Welbikes made at The Frythe, Old Welwyn] which used to be packed into containers and dropped into enemy-occupied countries. Such escapades caused us a severe ticking-off if we were caught. Sometimes there were bets about climbing the high water tower near a pub called The Green Man.[1]

Cyril Heath, a reporter for the *Herts and Essex Observer*, noted that local people had guessed that something was going on and had got to know some of the agents. Presumably they had gone into Hertford.

> One Hertfordian was told by three men training at Brickendonbury to listen to the news on a certain night. He did so and heard that 'French resistance workers had blown up Paris radio station'. Three days later he saw the three men again, and they gave him something which they said no-one else in England had. It was a ticket for the Folies Bergère – for that week![2]

Following Peters's resignation, his position as Brickendonbury's Commanding Officer was taken by forty-two-year-old Cecil 'Nobby' Clarke. During the First World War he had been an officer in the Pioneer Battalion in Italy and France engaged in tunnelling and explosives work, winning the Military Cross. In the 1920s and 30s he was the director of a motor engineering workshop in Bedford and was in correspondence with Stuart Macrae, the editor of *Armchair Science*. They had met before the war and Macrae decided that 'Nobby' might be able to help.

Although I had not seen him since this initial visit, Clarke's unusual personality and his ability to view mechanical problems in an unorthodox way had always stuck in my mind. I decided that he was the man for me, jumped into my motorcar complete with rough drawings and my collection of magnets, and went off to Bedford. I had of course rung up Clarke to warn him that I was coming and given him a very guarded idea of what I wanted to talk about. He was operating from his private house which he had converted in some remarkable way into a works. Sweeping a number of children out of his living room which had also to serve as an office, he filled me with bread and jam and some awful buns and then we got down to business. Nobby, as I soon came to call him, was enthusiastic as I knew he would be. 'Fine! How about starting tomorrow? Be here as early as you can. Stay here if you like; we can easily find you a bed.'[3]

This link extended throughout the Second World War and involved top-secret work for Winston Churchill and the Special Operations Executive's 'boffins' or 'backroom boys', scientists and technicians who were involved in the design and manufacture of top-secret weaponry. To assist him in his project, Clarke used the outbuildings behind the family home as an experimental workshop. His son John recalled him often being in the workshop during the first months of the war working on a limpet mine, a top-secret new weapon with enormous potential for the war effort.

When, in 1939, Macrae was asked by somebody in the War Office if he could assist with the procurement or getting information where such things could be procured, whether he could supply or find a supplier for limpets and he was not told initially what they were for. But after his security clearance had been established with the War Office, Macrae was told that the idea was to provide limpet mines that could sink enemy shipping. So he said, 'I will do my best to design something with a colleague of mine whom I know and the two of us together, I think we can produce something for the use of British Forces.'

He'd got a short time but as he said, he'd got 'a bag of gold' from the War Office to do everything that was necessary. He contacted my father and came down to Bedford and the two got on very well – they'd known each other before because of the caravan experience. They cleared all the children out of the room where they were discussing the matter and then started to get the design together. It was very much an ad hoc way of approaching the thing but both were brilliant at lateral thinking and the two men within about a month (this was in June/July 1939) before the war, had evolved a practicable Mark I type of limpet mine.

As the eldest boy, I was then 10 years old, I took a keen interest in what was going on and I knew broadly speaking what this was about. I was told not to say anything about it to my schoolboy friends. But the interesting thing about the limpet mine was that it was very much Bedford home-made. The two men visited Woolworths and they got washing up bowls made of spun aluminium to contain the explosives.[4]

Macrae recalled them cajoling a local tinsmith into stopping all the other work he was doing and fashioning some rims with annular grooves to fit the bowls and plates they had bought. These were then screwed in place to allow the rims to close.

The rims were sweated to the bowls and as many of the little horseshoe magnets as possible were packed into the annular grooves so that the pole pieces were exposed, these pole pieces then being lined up by simply placing a keeper ring over the whole lot. To secure the magnets in place we at first poured bitumen into the groove, but later found that plaster of Paris was a better answer.

The idea was to stuff this bowl full of blasting gelatin or some similar high explosive and then screw the lid in place so that the device was sealed. It had to be carried by a swimmer, so we contrived a belt consisting of a 4-inch-wide steel plate, just long enough to span the magnet ring, to which were attached strips of webbing which could be tied round the swimmer's waist. Obviously the swimmer must not be unduly handicapped by having to travel under water with this contrivance so we wanted it to weigh next to nothing when submerged. Eventually, after using up all the porridge in the house in place of high explosive for filling, juggling about with weights and dimensions, and flooding Nobby's bathroom on several occasions, we got this right.[5]

The field trials took place in Bedford Baths, about 200 yards away from the Clarke's household. Given the nature of their experiments, the baths were closed to the public during these tests. A large steel plate was propped up against the wall of the deep end to represent the side of a ship. Macrae appreciated Clarke being an excellent swimmer.

Looking as if he were suffering from advanced pregnancy, he would swim to and fro removing the device from his belt, turning it over, and plonking it on the target plate with great skill. We learned a lot more than when we had been in the bathroom. Our magnets were so powerful that when in the water it at first proved difficult to remove the mine from the keeper plate belt without the risk of rupturing oneself. So we had to experiment with various sizes of plate until we had one which gave the required hold and no more. The buoyancy too came in for adjustment as we found it advantageous to have slight positive buoyancy.[6]

John was often taken along to watch, and presumably to enjoy swimming in an otherwise empty pool. He recalled that,

A swimmer would be loaded up with the limpet mines before swimming to the side of a ship and plant the charge against the side using magnets on the underside of the limpet mine. Hence the curved shape with the magnets underneath it looked like a gigantic limpet when it was attached to the hull of a ship. My father gallantly undertook all these tests himself with a steel plate strapped around his tummy and the charge on the limpet mine attached to it. He had quite a lot of problems with adjusting the number of magnets to be used. If it was too strong you just couldn't get the thing off and were struggling underwater with a very heavy metal casing on your tummy.

There they were, swimming up and down and plonking them on a steel plate at the deep end and this worked well. Then to simulate the effect of a ship having had a limpet mine planted on it, all unsuspected, deciding to get underway and move through the water we had to ensure that the drag of the water on the limpet mine on the side of the hull wouldn't cause it to come away.

I remember going with my father in the motor boat and we trundled up and down the [River Great] Ouse at different speeds with this underwater device, which nobody could see because it was under the water. And we demonstrated that the launch could travel up to 10 or 15 knots and the limpet mine was still firmly attached. So that was yet another test that my father had to undergo and it was all extremely interesting and exciting. I would repeat that this was done just before the war started.[7]

Back at the workshop, Macrae christened it 'The Limpet'. What they hoped was that the enemy kept their ships in good condition as it would not stick to a hull covered in barnacles.

The next problem they had to solve was the 'delayed action initiator'. Various types had to be devised that would detonate the limpet after a delay of anywhere between half an hour and two hours after it was stuck on the ship. As there was nothing on the market at that time, they needed

a spring-loaded striker, maintained in the cocked position by a pellet soluble in water. When the pellet dissolved, the striker would be released to hit a cap to initiate a detonator which would explode a primer to explode the main charge. All this was easy enough, but finding a suitable pellet was difficult. There were too many variables. The powder itself was the first one, and the degree to which it was compressed the second one. The temperature of the water made all the difference, and of course so did whether it was fresh water or sea water. Expert chemists were called in to find us the answer, but they failed. One day a pellet would dissolve at a rate that alarmed us and would no doubt have alarmed a Limpeteer. The next day, a similar one might take several hours over the job and we did not want that. There was some hope of a Limpet staying put on a stationary target and every chance of its getting washed off if the target moved off at 20 knots or so as it might well do in time.

One of Nobby's children solved the problem for us. It was only a small one and, in sweeping it off the bench which it much preferred to its play pen, we upset it by knocking its bag of aniseed balls on to the floor. While Nobby was doing the consoling act, I tried one of these sweets. It seemed to stay with me a long time, getting smaller and smaller with great regularity. After trying a couple himself Nobby agreed that this might well be the answer so we commandeered the remainder of the supply and started to experiment. I think I can safely claim to be the first man to drill holes into aniseed balls and devise a fitting to enable this to be done accurately and efficiently. We rigged up some of our igniters with these aniseed balls in place of soluble pellets and the next day the children of Bedford had to go without their aniseed balls.[8]

It must have been quite exciting for John as he recalled having to visit all the sweet shops in Bedford and purchasing all their supplies of aniseed balls. Michael Simmonds, John's friend who lived opposite on Clarendon Street, recalled playing with him in his garden.

One day, I remember, he took us into his father's factory/workshop. We were very interested, of course, and wondered why there was someone, a lady, I think, drilling holes in aniseed balls. We were told that these were for making necklaces for children to suck in hospital! We believed this and were given the crumbs from the drillings to eat. Sweet rations were short, so we were glad of a little extra! Little did we know then that the aniseed balls were really for fuses for limpet mines

to be attached to enemy shipping! When the aniseed ball dissolved in
the sea water, it activated the bomb.[9]

Once the spring wire was threaded through the hole drilled through
the sweet, and the detonator was attached, the device was immersed
in water. When the aniseed ball completely dissolved, a time delay of
an hour or so, the detonator would set off the explosives. This allowed
the 'frogmen', saboteurs who were to attach the limpet mines to the
sides of enemy ships, a safe time to escape before the charges went off.
John recalled seeing

> quite a lot of this activity going on in the house, particularly this
> interesting development with an unusual use of aniseed balls. The
> aniseed balls were drilled and then they were put into little detonator
> capsules and my father had these ranged around the house and setting
> off at different times depending on the amount of aniseed ball that
> was used on each detonator. He would rush into the room in the
> house where, on the mantelpiece, one of these charges would be put
> in a big glass Woolworth's tumbler and he would say, 'Right, that's
> 35 minutes'. It didn't matter that probably the glass had fractured
> and all the water had gone – he had got something that worked and
> they were quickly able to establish how much of an aniseed ball was
> needed to give the varying times of delay that the operators would
> require.[10]

The device was tested at Bletchley Park and successfully blew a hole in
a stationary barge. The next step was an attempt to attach a limpet onto
a moving vessel. A dummy limpet was fixed with magnets to a police
launch on the Thames but it fell off. The magnetic system needed to be
improved.[11] Various modifications were made and Macrae pointed out
that,

> For safety's or danger's sake, we equipped each limpet with two of
> three delayed action exploders. The aniseed part of the device had
> of course to be protected from damp whilst it was in store – and in

fact until the Limpet was actually placed on its target. So what we needed was a closed rubber sleeve of some sort which could be pushed over the tube to seal it and whipped off by the Limpeteer when the time came. Again the local shops were able to meet the requirement. We went round to the chemists buying up all their stocks of a certain commodity and earning ourselves an undeserved reputation for being sexual athletes.[12]

During the winter of 1939 Clarke manufactured the first 250 limpets in his Tavistock Street workshop. When the second order was for 1,000, additional space was needed so he bought larger premises nearby.

Nobby and I had done a little costing work on Limpets. His overheads were pretty low, so the asking price came to something like £8 a time out of which he could afford to pay me £2 commission. This was probably more than the profit Nobby was making himself, but he was like that.[13]

As knowledge of the limpet's potential spread, further orders came from not just the SOE but also the Royal Marines and the Office of Strategic Services (OSS), the American equivalent of the SOE, who were running a similar training scheme for their saboteurs. As a result of the increased demand, Bassett's, the sweet manufacturers, were given the contract to supply their aniseed balls to a company in Welwyn, Hertfordshire, which was given the contract to manufacture limpets. By the time the war had ended, it had produced over half a million.

Another of Clarke's ideas attracted the attention of Winston Churchill. He had submitted a paper entitled 'A consideration of new offensive means', which outlined the design of a 60-foot-long, 140-ton, high-speed trench-forming machine. Described as 'a man of remarkable coincidences of ideas', in May 1940 he was appointed Assistant Director, Naval Land Section, Ministry of Supply, with a salary of £1,000 a year. Under the directorship of Mr Hopkins, Naval Constructor, his job was to complete the machine's design and construction. It had the capacity to advance through the Siegfried Line, heavily defended German defences running north–south along their border with Holland, Belgium and France. Clarke's plan was that it laid and fired explosive charges in front of itself so that it could make much quicker progress. He expected it to travel at 200 yards per hour and progress 3–4 miles in a night. The trench it formed, up to 10 feet wide and 8 feet deep, was big enough to accommodate tanks. A long artillery attack would be needed during its operation to drown out its noise. Plans were made to build a prototype, but on 25 June 1940 France's General Pétain surrendered to the Germans, which meant the target disappeared and the scheme was shelved.

Clarke immediately resigned from the Ministry of Supply and notified the War Office of his availability. Called up almost immediately, he signed the Official Secrets Act and was posted to the Intelligence Corps for special duty and joined the SOE staff at their Technical Research and Development Station at Aston House. Unlike Brickendonbury, the park was surrounded by a high wire fence and the locals were told that it was being used to test aircraft flares, special rockets for the Navy and special star-shell fillings for the Army. Its staff wore old civilian clothes and dark sunglasses and were all given fictitious names.

When Clarke first arrived 'to sort out a little problem with the Limpet mine', he did not create a very good impression with his superiors. Macrae mentioned that

> Nobby never did stand on ceremony. After waiting five minutes or so at the Guard Post he wandered off and contrived to avoid all security measures and get himself into the house and Langley's presence in another five minutes flat. Nobby relished this kind of exercise and specialised in it later on when he joined the Cloak and Dagger experts himself – first at this station E.S.6 [Experimental Station] and later as O.C. [Officer in Command] of one at Hertford [Brickendonbury]. But although Langley belonged to the same Senior Service he would not wear this one at all. Next day I received a note from him deploring the conduct on behalf of an officer for whom I was responsible. In future, he said, would I please send some officer

with some sense of responsibility to Aston House on these missions. If I again sent Captain Clarke he might be admitted to the grounds of Aston House to carry out such work as the testing of Limpets but in no circumstances would he be allowed inside the house and he could not be served with meals. Langley went off a few months later to take a more active part in the war at sea and Nobby then did get into the house for meals. In fact he lived there for several months, having been taken on the strength by Commander Langley's successor – Captain L. J. C. Wood.[14]

When Gubbins got to hear about Clarke and his exploits, he considered him the ideal candidate for running Brickendonbury. In December 1940, promoted to Captain (Acting Major), Clarke was appointed Officer in Charge. Code-named D/DP, he was entrusted with overseeing the sabotage training. In an SOE folder entitled Training Lectures and Statistics, possibly written by Clarke, it points out that explosives and detonators were to be termed 'sweets' and 'toys' and that 'Sabotage, explosives, detonators and propaganda material in "our business"' were taboo terms.[15] According to Macrae, training saboteurs

> was just Nobby's cup of tea and enabled him to become a bigger menace. He had no security guards on the gates of his magnificent estate. One just drove in and then found the vehicle being battered by rounds fired by spigot mortars set off by trip wires. Nobby emerged smiling and pointed out that if they had been live rounds the occupants of the vehicle would no longer be with us. But that was of little consolation to the driver who had to explain how the bodywork of his vehicle had been badly bashed.[16]

In the memoirs of Lieutenant Denis Newman, one of the demolition instructors, one of Clarke's entertainments is mentioned:

> The main parting demonstration for visiting dignitaries was to have an old car towed down the drive with a suitable length of rope, giving

the driver some protection, and then a spigot mortar would be fired by a tripwire. It was a nice avenue of tall trees down the approach to Brickendonbury and these were prettily decorated with bits of old car as a result of these demonstrations of the spigot mortar. It was quite impressive.[17]

Clarke felt it very important that the enthusiastic foreign volunteers should get some actual hands-on experience of trying to carry out an attack. His son's memoirs describe how

my father made out a pass on War Office paper saying: 'The holder of this pass, Major C. V. Clarke, has authority to inspect Luton Power Station.' So armed with this pass, which I'm sure from judging the signature which looked remarkably like my father's, he took his team from Hertford to Luton one dark night. They used scaling ladders to get over the walls of Luton Power Station, which of course was guarded like all big installations. They successfully got inside, planted dummy charges on all the transformers, and then got back over the wall successfully without anybody noticing. They, having cleared off to a nearby street and waited for my father who then walked up to the front door of the power station which of course was under guard and asked for the Officer of the guard and produced his pass and he said, 'I want to do a routine inspection.' So he went round with a very big torch and he came up to the first transformer and he flashed his torch and he said, 'What's that?' And this young Subaltern who was in charge of the guard, 'I'm not quite sure what this is Sir.' 'It looks to me like an explosive charge. Let's have a look round.' And in the end the poor Subaltern in charge of the guard was knocked kneed with what he'd let happen. So my father, who was a kindly man said, 'Alright old man, you say nothing about this and I'll say nothing about it. But you've learnt your lesson.' With that he had his team back to retrieve the appliances and off they went. But this was very valuable training, slightly unorthodox but it's one of those things that happened in war time. One of the more wilder outfits in the Army during the war![18]

Philby described Clarke as having a 'rumbustious' sense of humour. When he was asked to arrange a demonstration of his skills to the Czech Director of Military Intelligence and his staff,

> he planted booby traps in a copse through which they had to walk to his training-ground. He had assumed they would go through the wood in Indian file like ducks. Instead they walked abreast, and the officers at each end of the line suffered nasty shocks. It was a fluke nobody got hurt.[19]

Among the nationalities John recalled his father training were Poles, Frenchmen and Dutchmen. Sometimes he provided them with a brief respite.

> I remember as an example of my father's trust in me because I had an uncle who had a farm out at Pulloxhill in Bedfordshire. My father, shortly before an operation was due to take place and before a group of saboteurs were sent off, they having been trained up to the limit and needing a couple of days' break, were sent by my father across to Pulloxhill to help bring in the harvest or do some other job on the farm and it happened that I was there at the same time. My father told me that these foreign people who were on the farm helping my uncle, were saboteurs, that they were going to be dropped over Europe but they were not to know under any circumstances that I was Major Clarke's son. So we kept absolutely quiet about that and worked with them in the field as they were having their break before going on their dangerous missions.[20]

Another weapon 'Nobby' was involved with was the 'Sticky Bomb'. This was a grenade that could be thrown at a tank and would stick to it for five seconds or so and then explode, blowing a hole in its side and, in Macrae's words, 'disconcert the occupants'. There was also the 'W' Bomb, manufactured at Midgely Harmer's engineering works in the Park Royal industrial estate in Wembley, North London. This was a mine designed to be dropped by an aircraft into a river and sink to the bed and remain dormant for a predetermined period. It would then rise to just below the surface and float with the current until it came into contact with a boat or a ship whereupon it would explode with sufficient force to produce a wreck. If it failed to explode after a certain time, it would sink to the bottom and become harmless.

The 'Kangaroo Bomb' and the 'Johnnie Walker Bomb' were variants on this. Upon entering the water, the bomb was expected to dive underwater then surface. This would be repeated until it struck the relatively less protected underside of a ship at which point the 90-pound Torpex warhead would explode.[21]

Clarke also liaised with the Imperial Chemicals Industries Limited who were involved in the design and manufacture of high explosives and the filling of shells and mortars. One of their inventions that was of interest to Clarke was 'a little 1.7 grain detonator which was only about the size of a percussion cap but instead of needing a blow of 3 in/lb to set it off only had to be prodded lightly with a needle point'.[22] These were used in the 'Clam', a much smaller and more portable version of the Limpet. Macrae claimed that it was their second-best seller and that,

for the Cloak and Dagger boys it was God's Gift from Heaven. They could carry these things in their pockets and just stick them to something they would like to blow up. Although the explosive content was only around 8 ounces, ICI produced some very high speed stuff for us and the design was such that the explosive was almost in contact with the target over a considerable area. A Clam could put any motor vehicle out of commission or an aero engine for that matter. But its success was dependant on the use of the 'L' Delay which was made part of it. If operators had had to use it with a Time Pencil they would not have been so enthusiastic about it. My diary is full of notes of people squealing for Clams. The Russians had nearly a million of them and were always asking for more. The total number of Clams made under MDI surveillance during the war was over two and a half million.[23]

Macrae used these tiny detonators to produce what he called 'M'-Mines, small explosive devices that he was able to produce at five shillings a time. The ICI detonators were also used in shells designed for another of Clarke's projects, the design and development of the projector for the 'Projector, Infantry, Anti-Tank (PIAT)' gun. Although he designed a silencing attachment for the propellant cartridge, the Director General did not consider this necessary when the weapon was used by regular troops.

> It consisted of a steel tube, a trigger mechanism and firing spring, and was based on the spigot mortar system; instead of using a propellant to directly fire a round, the spring was cocked and tightened. When the trigger was pulled, it released the spring which pushed the spigot forward into the rear of the bomb. This detonated the propellant in the bomb itself, which was then thrown forward off the spigot. It possessed an effective range of approximately 100 yards (90 m).
>
> This system meant that the PIAT had several advantages, which included a lack of muzzle smoke to reveal the position of the user, the ability to fire it from inside buildings, and an inexpensive barrel; however, this was countered by, amongst other things, a difficulty in cocking the weapon, the bruising the user received when firing it, and problems with its penetrative power.[24]

It was SOE policy for its officers to undertake the same training as the agents. This was also the case with the staff at Brickendonbury. Accordingly, in June 1941, Clarke was sent to Manchester where he attended a parachute course at Ringway Aerodrome. This usually involved five days learning how to jump from increasing heights, land and roll without hurting oneself, put on ankle supports, padded clothing and a 'sorbet' rubber hat, attach the harness and parachute and then make three practice jumps from an air balloon at about 500 feet before making two from a converted Whitley Bomber over the nearby Tatton Park. To add realism, one had to be at night.[25]

To assist Clarke, on 10 December 1941 a second instructor was appointed. This was forty-year-old William Blackden, an engineering graduate who had been working in Finland as a representative for Metropolitan-Vickers Electric Company. Fluent in Finnish and Swedish and able to speak some French and German, he was described as having 'a clever brain' and being an excellent instructor, particularly in the case of the more intelligent students. Other reports stated that he had 'a likeable personality with a sound sense of responsibility', 'considerable technical knowledge', 'popular in the mess' but having 'little knowledge of Army administration'.[26]

When Clarke was not demonstrating or developing explosives, he wrote the 'Blue Book', a manual on sabotage techniques, used by the SOE. Included were instructions on how to use a 'Tree Spigot', a new light weapon he had invented and produced prototypes for. The existing mortar-firing gun had such powerful recoil and his modifications so improved its effectiveness that the Americans purchased large quantities. Their Field Photographic Unit produced an instructional film for agents in the Office of Strategic Services (OSS), the United States' intelligence agency, in which it told them that

The spigot gun was a booby trap or saboteurs' weapon for attack against both moving and stationary and moving targets. It is very light and portable and capable of throwing a comparatively heavy bomb with accuracy up to 250 yards. The equipment for spigot gun operation consists of the spigot, the base of the gun, sights for aiming the gun and the bomb which is projected at the target. The spigot has an augur-like handle for setting into the tree or other substantial support and one of the handles is chiselled for scraping away bark. The spigot rod is mounted in the base in a ball and socket joint so it may be aimed and elevated as required. A clamp holds it firmly in the aimed position. The rod contains a spring actuated striker which is held in cocked position by the end of a trip wire inserted in the hole between rod and striker. The sight, similar in principle to a view finder on a camera has range scales in both metres and yards. It fits on the spigot rod while the operator centres the gun on the target before the bomb is attached. The bomb which sits over the spigot rod and is projected to the target is made up of three parts – tail, head and fuse.

In the tail there is a shot-gun type of cartridge which when hit by the firing pin of the spigot rod supplies the driving force of the bomb. The silencing rod keeps gases, flames and smoke inside the tail of the bomb making the point of firing very difficult to locate. When the striker in the spigot rod is released by removing the trip wire it springs forward to hit the cartridge in the bomb tail. The exploding cartridge drives the bomb off the rod and the silencing rod and shell peel themselves in the end of the tail preventing the escape of noise and fire. The initial acceleration arms the special fuse so that when the bomb hits its target the impact drives the fuse firing pin into a detonating cap which ignites the booster charge. This booster charge in turn detonates the three pounds of plastic explosive carried in the bomb head.[27]

Time pencils could be inserted when the saboteur felt that they did not need to be present when the vehicle, locomotive, oil storage tank or building was hit. His 'Plate Spigot' was the same but attached to the gun was a bulletproof steel plate that screened the firer. Both these weapons were taken on by E.S.6, the War Office, as they could also be used by the Home Guard should a German invasion ever take place. He also designed a light, portable explosive road trap that was successfully used by SOE and OSS agents. Exactly what it was was not specified but, to give you an idea, the SOE's 'backroom boys' concealed explosives in cavities inside actual everyday objects or in life-size replicas made of plaster or celluloid. These included exploding rusty nuts and bolts, wooden clogs, Chianti wine bottles, screw-top milk bottles, fountain pens, railway fishplates, oilcans, lifebelts, bicycle pumps, food tins, candles, soap, shaving brushes, books, loaves of bread, lumps of coal, rock, turnips, beetroots, stuffed mice and rats and even cow, horse, mule and camel dung!

Most mornings at Brickendonbury began with PT, Physical Training. Their instructors included Lieutenant Francis, sergeants Redhouse and Carter and a Mr Jarret, who had been head waiter at the Royal Victoria Hotel in Hastings. Sue Ryder described Jarret as 'a bit of a leg-puller. One of his pet expressions was "I don't know what will happen to us all."'[28]

Until the SOE introduced paramilitary training in agents' courses in the area around Arisaig, north-west Scotland, after parachute training at Ringway, those identified as needing sabotage training were sent to Brickendonbury. On 1 January 1942, Major Bill Sykes, an ex-Shanghai policeman in his late fifties, was brought in to help. A silver-haired, round-rimmed-spectacled man with a neat centre parting, he was an expert in pistol shooting and silent killing. His students described him as looking more like a portly bishop than an athletic army captain. He provided lessons in what was called 'ungentlemanly warfare'.

What he wanted students to do from the outset was what he described as 'unlearning the game of cricket'. The warfare he taught at Brickendonbury, and later in Scotland, was part Chinese boxing and part premeditated murder. His philosophy was that Great Britain and the Commonwealth were facing utterly ruthless killers and it was now down to the elemental maxim: 'Kill or be killed'. Should it come down to one-to-one combat, only one person would walk away. They had to make sure that it was them. Either they kill or capture, or they would be captured or killed. Students reported him telling them about the phrase 'the quick and the dead'; if you didn't fire first, you'd be shot. 'Shoot to live' was another of his exhortations. What was found surprising was that he spoke in soft, dulcet tones and had a benevolent smile. Apart from kneeing your opponent in the testicles and grinding your boot into his ankle, he taught them some remarkable ways of using matchboxes, umbrellas, pens and pencils as offensive weapons. They practiced jabbing them into the eye sockets, ears or nose of straw-filled dummy heads. In Marcus Binney's *Secret War Heroes*, he quotes Leslie Fernandez, one of ten future sabotage instructors, describing Sykes as

'a likeable man, quiet yet dynamic too, suddenly bursting into action ... He knew all about pressure points, how to paralyse a man in an instant.' He also provided extensive instruction on illegal entry and escape. 'For example, he devised a system of scaling twelve-foot barbed wire enclosures with overhangs. It was very difficult to get through barbed-wired fences without cutting the wire and setting off alarms. He invented a pair of stirrups, each with a hook on the back. You would put all your weight on one foot and then left the other.'[29]

Sykes's general theory lessons were in one of the rooms and the practice sessions were outside on the lawn. Using flip charts and live volunteers, he showed them exactly where to apply pressure on different parts of the body, how much, what with and for how long. Elbows, hands, fingertips, knees, toes and heels could be deadly if used properly. The karate chop, using the side of the hand between your little finger and wrist, can burst blood vessels, shatter bones, paralyse and kill. Carefully placed hits at the side of the temple, the base of the neck, anywhere from the nose to the throat, on either side of the spine, the kidneys, upper arm or forearm could be lethal. They were encouraged to use little karate chops on the edge of tables, the tops of chairs, the sides of doors, anything to fracture the bone so that it regrew even stronger. They were shown where to kick someone on the head if they were down and they did not want them to get up. There are places where the spinal column is very vulnerable. Obviously they only practiced these lethal jabs and thrusts on dummies. The names they used were quite apt – 'The Bear Hug', 'The Bronco Kick' and 'The Back Breaker'. They were taught to fall properly, slapping the palm of your hand onto the ground first to reduce the impact. During wrestling lessons, they were encouraged to put their finger in the opponent's mouth and then rip the cheek open. No doubt some of the students used his training in the field.

Another clandestine subject reported as being taught at Brickendonbury was burglary. Breaking into a factory by and large meant having to cut through perimeter fences, maybe forcing gates, doors and windows. Learning how to do so without making a lot of noise and without attracting attention were vital skills that students needed teaching as well as those of sabotage.

An ex-burglar taught a course in lock-forcing and safe-breaking. During the courses it was impressed on the agents that their task was aggressive, that they must make aggression part of their characters, eat with it, sleep with it, live with it, absorb it into themselves.

They were taught to be self-reliant, to accept disappointment, patient in waiting for an opening, always ready to pounce on any chance, however fleeting, to harm the enemy ... Towards the end of the war the station had perfected a sophisticated technique which consisted of getting factory owners to sabotage their own factories. An agent would approach an owner and say something like this: 'Why don't you sabotage your own factory? You can do it in such a way that at the end of the war you can get it working again with the minimum of delay.' But the sting in the tail: 'Unless you do we will call in the RAF to flatten your factory.'[30]

There were lighter moments. Len Macey recalled that he and Tom Long were sent to Brickendonbury prior to naval operations with the Helford Flottila in Brittany over the winter of 1940/1. While they underwent the sabotage course, he most remembered the unarmed combat course.

We went to this vast house in the country and the first thing in the morning we were told to report to the Army drill shed or some such place. There was a sergeant standing on a great big mattress there and he said, 'I want you to run at me and knock me over', and we thought this a bit funny. He said, 'Come on. Don't hang about.' So I went at him and the next thing I was flying over his head ... It was that kind of thing that happened at Brickendonbury and then they taught us to use the yellow plastic explosive. Tom and I had to crawl around Hertfordshire ... putting it on train lines and pretending that we were blowing up trains. We never blew them up, of course, but I still don't know whether the stuff was fake or not.[31]

Macey also mentioned meeting William Fairburn, known as 'Shanghai Buster', Sykes's partner in ungentlemanly warfare training. They developed what was called the F. & S. knife, specially designed for murder. Maybe Fairburn helped out at Brickendonbury before they were transferred to Scotland, as Macey also recalled,

> We had a fellow come down and they said, 'He's the unarmed combat expert and he will show you a few things.' This guy came aboard and said, 'Get a chair, please,' so I went and got a chair ... and he sat someone in it and the next moment he's got his arm around his neck and he's got a knife in. He said, 'Do you know I'm just showing you how easy it is to kill a person.' So a couple of days he showed us all kinds of things – how to kill with two fingers or hit them in certain places ... He didn't look like a killer at all or a policeman, but he was a great expert.[32]

There was also weapon training using Thompson and Browning sub-machine guns, Bren guns and Sten guns, a French machine gun and a Schmeisser, the German equivalent. They were shown how to take them apart, how to put them back together again and how to load them. Then they had to fire them, lying down, kneeling, standing up and then while running. In the evening, after a meal, they would be given machine guns, the lights would be turned off and they had to dismantle them in the dark. Having done that, they had to remount them. To speed them up they were offered a prize of a 'ten-bob' note. George Howard provided intensive training in small arms, getting the students to improve their shooting skills using revolvers, the Colt automatic and Lugers, small Belgian pistols.

In April 1942 Clarke asked for and was given a transfer to help Macrae at the Firs, another requisitioned country house at Whitchurch near Aylesbury in Buckinghamshire. His knowledge and expertise was needed in the design and manufacture of what was called the 'Altimeter Switch' or 'Aero Switch'. This was a small sabotage device that could be inserted into an enemy plane by some brave saboteur and would explode when the aircraft reached a certain height. Clarke's idea was that the saboteur, dressed as a worker in the aircraft factory, would have a flexible sausage of explosive hidden in a trouser pocket so that it would not attract any comments. Macrae said that

He was wrong about the 'without comment' and there was always considerable ribaldry when he demonstrated this method to his pupils. But actually it was sound common sense and I believe they all adopted it.

In due course we went into production at Whitchurch with this Aero Switch and made and issued many thousands of them. Later by special request we managed to get the operational height down to 5,000 feet without sacrificing the saboteur's safety. The usual drill was to make a slit in the wing fabric of a German bomber and pop this thing inside so that in due course the wing would be wrecked.[33]

The Firs, code-named MDI, was a unit in Whitchurch responsible for the design, development and production of special munitions and the training of Special Forces in their use. Macrae referred to it as 'Winston Churchill's toyshop'.

Clarke's position as Brickendonbury's Commanding Officer was taken by forty-year-old Major George Rheam, who has been described as the founder of modern industrial sabotage. Born in Liverpool in 1900, after getting a BSc in electrical engineering, he worked for eight years with Metropolitan-Vickers, a heavy electrical engineering company in Manchester, well-known for their industrial electrical equipment such as steam turbines, generators, switchgears, transformers, electronics and railway traction equipment. From 1930 he worked as an engineer at the North Metropolitan Power Company's power station at Southgate in London and was in charge of its design and construction. In 1938 he worked in the Anti-Aircraft division workshop at Uxbridge and in February 1939 was commissioned as Deputy Assistant Director of Ordnance Services (Engineering) in the 1st Anti-Aircraft Corps with a rank as Major. By this time he was married with two children and was living in Barnet.[34]

In 1941, little was known about the most effective ways of using explosives to blow up buildings or destroy machinery. Rheam's knowledge and expertise in industrial engineering drew him to the attention of the SOE and, three weeks after being recruited, on 24

August 1941, Gubbins appointed him as Brickendonbury's instructor in industrial sabotage.

A note in his personnel file stated that 'he is in a position to contact firms in this country with a view to getting detailed information and, if the need arises, getting employment at special terms for our trainees'.[35] When Clarke left Brickendonbury, Rheam took over on 23 November 1942 and was promoted to Lieutenant-Colonel. Foot described him as

> a large man with a large mind, the inventor of many industrial sabotage techniques and an instructor of genius. He had that rare combination, accurate hands and a highly imaginative brain. Those who did exactly what he told them never had a cause to regret it. Bridette Bardot's film *Babette Goes to War* took him off as a figure of fun; the Germans thought him anything but funny.
>
> He was a tall man with steady grey eyes; his pupils tended to think him dour. He was not much given to suffering fools gladly, and knew rather better than most of them the rigidities of the systems they were trying to conquer. His friends knew that behind his stiffish manner lay a keen sense of humour, as well as intense sympathy for the exiles from the European continent with whom he often worked.[36]

Unlike many of SOE's leading figures who had never done anything more mechanical than change a wheel or replace spark plugs on a car, Rheam had a background in what he taught. According to Foot, 'He ran a thoroughly serious business, based on common sense.'[37]

In Rheam's personnel file, Lieutenant Colonel Spooner described him as 'an officer whose technical, industrial and administrative ability is of the highest order. He is most thorough and conscientious being as he is absorbed in his technical work, is inclined to be unsympathetic towards the human side of his subordinate officers ... Not very broadminded, not easy to get to know – nevertheless very round and reliable.' Gubbins described him as 'a very able officer, who is an expert in his type of training.' Colonel Young described him as 'a strong, dour, efficient officer, who does not easily brook any outside apparent interference.'[38]

Part of the grounds were turned into a demolition research area and, probably with Rheam's help, factories and scrap yards over a wide area were searched for suitable machinery and plant to experiment on. The North British Locomotive company loaned him a model of a steam engine on which to show students exactly where to place their explosives.[39] Later the students had opportunities to blow them up. As well as industrial areas, electrical installations, power stations, dams, airfields, canals, railways and the telegraph networks were targeted. To assist the students in this work, Ryder said that the school had three planes, 'a two-engined Manchester, a Tempest or Typhoon with a Sabre engine and a German JU88. In addition it also had a Churchill tank, and all stood on the East drive with a GWR [Great Western Railway] locomotive in a nearby siding'.

A general course of three weeks' duration was devised to ensure as far as possible that every man not only had sufficient knowledge to operate efficiently and with confidence but also to act in turn as an instructor when he went into the field. There were also specialist courses and courses associated with a particular target.[40]

PROGRAMME OF WORK[41]

INDUSTRIAL SABOTAGE COURSE NO.   Week 1   Week Ending

	MONDAY	TUESDAY	WEDNESDAY	THURSDAY	FRIDAY	SATURDAY	SUNDAY
09.00-10.00		P.T.	P.T.	Weapons Training	P.T.	P.T.	
10.00-11.00		Organisation of Industry	Repairs to Machinery	Common Machinery II	Electrical Machinery I	Demolition of Machinery	Visit to Electric Substation
11.15-12.00		Factory Organisation	Lubrication	Distribution of Electric Power II	Common Machinery IV	Electrical Machinery II	=oo=
12.00-12.15		=oo=	Passive Resistance. General Principles	=oo=	=oo=	=oo=	=oo=
14.00-15.00		Demolition Exercise	Demolition I	Demolition II	Visit to Pumping Stat.	Preparation for Pumping Sta. Scheme	Practical Machinery
16.15-17.15	ASSEMBLY	Demolition Methods	Common Machinery I	Common Machinery III	=oo=	=oo=	FREE
17.15-18.15		Machinery	Distribution of Elec. Power	Telecommunications	Discussion on Visit	FREE	
EVENING	Commandant's Talk						Pumping Sta. N. Rd Scheme

INDUSTRIAL SABOTAGE COURSE NO.

PROGRAMME OF WORK

Week 2   Week Ending

	MONDAY	TUESDAY	WEDNESDAY	THURSDAY	FRIDAY	SATURDAY	SUNDAY
09.00-10.00	P.T.	P.T.	Weapons Training	P.T.	Visit to Iron & Steel Works	Discussion on Iron & Steel Visit	
10.00-11.00	Electrical Machinery III	Power Station Plant II.	Railway Rolling Stock	Iron and Steel Industry	=oo=	Machinery revision	Discussion on Railway Scheme
11.15-12.00	Transport Gen. Considerations	=oo=	=oo=	Coke Oven Plant	=oo=	Telecommunications II	Demolition Results
12.00-12.15	=oo=	Steam Power Size. General Considerations	Steel Wire stores	Blast Furnaces	=oo=	=oo=	=oo=
14.00-15.00	Practical Telecommunications	Visit to Power Station	Visit to Running Sheds & Coal wagons	Demolition III	=oo=	Preparation for Railway Scheme (Running Sheds)	Pumping Sta. (P.E.) Exercises
16.15-17.15	Generation of Electric Power (by sizes)	=oo=	=oo=	Steel Furnaces & Rolling Mills	=oo=	=oo=	FREE
17.15-18.15	Power Station I.	Discussion on Visit	=oo=	Electrical Revision	=oo=	=oo=	
EVENING	Commandant's Talk	Discussion on Visit	Discussion on Visit	Railway Exercise		Running Sheds Scheme	Pumping Sta. N. Rd Scheme

PROGRAMME OF WORK

INDUSTRIAL SABOTAGE COURSE NO.   Week 3   Week Ending

	MONDAY	TUESDAY	WEDNESDAY	THURSDAY	FRIDAY	SATURDAY	SUNDAY
09.00-10.00	P.T.	P.T.	Docks Equipment	Weapons Training	P.T.	Revision	
10.00-11.00	Incendiaries	Engineering Factories	Visit to Docks and Canals (5) & (6)	Machinery Revision	Foundries and Forges	Review of Course (?)	
11.15-12.00	Coal Mines	Machines Tools	=oo=	Oil Storage	=oo=	Telecommunications II	
12.00-12.15	=oo=	=oo=	=oo=	Aircraft Factories	Engineering Factories	=oo=	
14.00-15.00	Practical Machinery	Visit to small Engineering Factory	=oo=	Visit to Aircraft Factory	Visit to larger Engineering Factory	END OF COURSE	
16.15-17.15	Railway Goods Handling	=oo=	=oo=	=oo=	=oo=		
17.15-18.15	Canals	Discussion on Visit	=oo=	Discussion on Visit	Discussion on Visit		
EVENING	Demolition IV		Discussion on Visit				

In Michael Foot's *The SOE in France*, he described Rheam's course as 'famous,' including the theory and practice of industrial sabotage. It comprised of lectures, visits to industrial plants to enable students to identify the 'vital targets', practical work in the school grounds, on the local Metropolitan Water Board pumping station, the engine sheds at Hitchin, the local railway, and the nearby RAF Radlett and at the night-fighter base at Stansted.

Rheam taught his pupils how to look over a factory, and, within a few minutes, locate the few machines on which the whole plant depended. Then, by doing something simple such as hitting the cast-iron base once, hard, with a sledgehammer, he showed them how a vital machine could be put out of action. As Foot said, 'If you couldn't find a cover for carrying a sledgehammer on to a factory floor with you, what were you doing trying to work in SOE?'[42] Fracturing ironwork might have worked on some machinery, but on others much greater force was needed. This was where explosives became necessary and the students needed to be taught exactly how to use it.

Experiments with plastic explosive began in the Royal Arsenal at Greenwich just before the start of the war and the SOE was its first large-scale user. It had all sorts of clandestine advantages: it did not smell, it was readily mouldable into any required shape, and it was stable – it did not go off when jolted by anything less than a detonator.

When Clarke left, the demolition instructor at Brickendonbury was Sergeant England. Students on his course recall being thrown greaseproof paper parcels and expected to catch them. On unwrapping them they were told that the reddish-brown, soft, rubbery substance was 'a Nobel invention'. Some referred to it as '808', 'plasticine', *plastique* or, inexplicably, 'stagger juice'. It looked like butter; it stank of almonds, far stronger than marzipan, and left a distinct odour on their hands. When dropped to the ground, nothing happened. When kicked, nothing happened. When thrown into a fire, nothing happened. One student recalled being shocked when, squashed against a rock, the instructor took out his revolver and before he could react, shot it. Still nothing happened. It did not explode as expected. It just had a big splash of a bullet hole in it. In an emergency it could be burned as a fuel. Should they want to hide it, it could be used instead of putty to hold glass in a window. It lasted indefinitely. One Yugoslav trainee was said to have mashed it with milk to make what he thought was maize porridge and a subaltern in the SAS was said to have eaten some in the dark, thinking it was chocolate. It was not recommended. What effect it had on the human digestive system was not known but great uproar ensued when someone suggested that it might cause explosive farting.

Students would have been reassured to learn that it was not dangerous, as long as it was kept cool. It would not explode if hit by a rifle bullet or when dropped accidentally. You could cut it into different sized lumps and mould it into shapes, but it was only when it was really warmed up that it became highly explosive. Keeping it in your trouser pocket kept it soft, making it much easier to mould round the object you wanted to destroy. It was stressed that it was not cutting explosive like dynamite. It was best used for melting steel but to make it, it needed tamping. Tamping for railway lines; tamping for electricity generators; tamping for railway pistons; tamping for practically everything except trip wires and booby traps. All it needed was a primer, time pencils and detonating cord. How to set it off was what the students had to learn.

As a spur, a whisky was offered to anyone who could place a pull switch, press switch or self-opening switch on any part of the building, on any item of furniture in it or any of the boats that would detonate before Rheam found it. None of them got one. He seemed to have an uncanny ability to detect anything that could be wrong, as if he had a sixth sense and expected something to be there.

At the end of one session, he unpacked another detonator, which, he stressed, was not to be carried in the hand. Body warmth would set it off. It was made with fulminate of mercury. Previous recruits, he told them, had had their hands or fingers blown off by not handling it properly. It needed packing carefully if they were to use it in the field. Hiding it in their beret was probably the safest bet, just in case they fell over and banged it accidentally. They believed him.

While some of the students were trained for specific missions, what was stressed again and again was that the knowledge and skills they learned were transferable. They needed to be able to teach others how to use them. What must have been awkward though was being told that the Germans were known to tie captives to the front of the locomotives to deter *derailleurs*.

Demonstrations were done on sheet metal out in the grounds, but, once shown how to prepare and shape the correct amount of explosive and insert the appropriate fuse, they had to learn the procedure off by heart before moving on to the practical work. Once the explosive was strapped on with sticky tape, they had to ensure that the instantaneous fuse was hanging correctly. The detonator needed to be attached to the time pencil and inserted into the hole they had made in the mould and the explosive pressed around it to stop it from falling out. Only then were they to bend the time pencil so as to break the glass containing the acid.

There were quarry trucks, excavators, conveyor belts, tramways, narrow gauge railways, coal-fired and electric pumping engines, electricity transformers, office buildings, stores, pylons and telegraph poles to choose from. They were told never to blow up all four legs of a pylon – they would just sink a few feet rather than topple over – three did the trick. And never to blow anything up that had trees nearby as, again, they did not completely collapse.

Choosing the right spot could paralyse the enemy war machine for an indefinite period. Choosing a cutting to blow up a goods train would block the line better than on flat land. Blowing up a troop train was better on high land when the carriages rolled down the hill or mountainside; they would kill more *Boches*. Avoid targeting trains with locals on; their support was needed, not their animosity.

Concerted, coordinated attacks would be good for demoralising the enemy and its collaborators and raising that of the Resistance. In some machinery it was a piston, a valve or a cylinder they had to target; in others it might be a conveyor belt or an electricity generator. It was the expert's job to recognise it quickly, if necessary in the dark, even though the threat of detection turned their fingers into thumbs.

Students recalled how they attached their first explosive on an old railway line, moulded a 2-pound lump around the 'T' of the rail, smoothed it over so that it wouldn't be visible unless on close inspection, stuck the fuse in, crimped it and, as instructed, walked calmly away. Two minutes later there was a loud bang and, when they went back to see what they had done, it had been neatly cut through like a knife slicing wartime margarine. The 3-inch gap was enough to derail a small train. However, two charges, about 18 inches apart, would derail a 50-ton engine. If it was a multiple railway, setting a charge on the other line about 200–300 yards away would avoid the explosion displacing the other.

Taken into the kitchen, they would have been shown the *bain marie*, the large tin used for steaming salmon. The explosive was placed inside it to warm up. They were also given practice at softening 808 under their armpits. Afterwards they were told that this method should only be used as a last resort as, over time, the oil soaks into the skin. Side effects included high temperatures, intense headaches and nausea. The other bad news was that the almond smell could be detected in your sweat for at least twenty-four hours afterwards. The good news was that the sickness would have worn off by then.

They would also have been shown the most recent explosive, RDX, safer than 808 and more powerful. The 'cookery lessons' also included some high-powered recipes for making bombs that could be used for blowing up bridges, derailing railway trains, trucks and carriages, destroying boilers, bringing down pylons and putting electricity transformers out of operation. Take half a pound of this, a few ounces of that, a tube of Bostic glue, a bag of magnets, sticky brown paper, sticky tape, greaseproof paper, a balloon and pincer pliers, mix them all together and – hey presto! – a sausage explosive.

Rheam stressed that a few ounces of well-placed plastic explosive could disable a factory. He stressed that if several machines were to be destroyed, it was best to destroy the same part on each machine. This would prevent repairs by what was called 'cannibalisation', replacing the part with one from another machine.

Francis Cammaerts, one of SOE's F Section organisers, attended what he called the 'Explosives School' at Brickendonbury and stated that apart from the joy of realising a boyhood dream of learning to drive a real railway engine on real rails, the course was enormously valuable because it dealt with steam and hydro-electric power stations, transmission systems, engineering factories, steam and electric railways and road transport, all of which would form part of my initial brief in Provence.

He described Rheam as 'a large man with a large mind, the inventor of many industrial sabotage techniques and an instructor of genius'.[43]

In Stafford's *Secret Agent*, Cammaerts recalled learning how to block the enemy's railway system by blowing up railway lines and sabotaging railway engines.

> I learnt about the use of very small quantities of explosives to destroy very important parts of machines, the kind of parts of machines which were irreplaceable or would take a very long time to replace. Those are the kinds of thing which were very important and which people like myself knew nothing about at all.[44]

Frank Gleason, an OSS demolition instructor, reported being sent to an industrial sabotage school in England, undoubtedly Brickendonbury.

> Six or seven people that are properly trained can cripple a good-sized city. It's as easy as can be. These terrorists scare me. If they know this stuff, which I'm sure they do, it's really easy to cripple a medium-sized city with trained demolitionists and arsonists. We learned how to operate and destroy locomotives and power plants, the turbines in power plants, communication systems, and telephones. We also learned how to make people sick by poisoning the city's water supply. Shitty stuff like that – we were taught to fight dirty.[45]

Tom Ellen recalled his father telling him that, while at Brickendonbury, he learned about the use of sand in the grease in locomotive wheel boxes, removing fishplates and chair wedges from rail track, removing wheel wedges and brakes on parked rolling stock to block tracks, and the carborundum powder.[46]

In my enquiries on the SOE user group on yahoo.com, Tom Colville told me that his father had trained at Brickendonbury. So far as he was able to determine, the training was in the correct use of explosives, industrial sabotage, the identification of critical industrial components and stress points in engineered structures. The training included various methods for rendering heavy machinery, rolling stock, points and signalling systems and rail track unusable. Not all the training was of an explosive nature. It included introducing carborundum paste and powder into wheel boxes and contaminating gearboxes and engines. As ball bearings were in critically short supply, this would put machinery out of action for long periods. Tampering with fuel lines, using time pencils and delayed-action switches on incendiaries were all silent things that allowed the operative to evade capture. He believed that

> the use of minimal and economical force was one of the ideas that came from Brickendonbury training. If operatives always disabled the right side undercarriage of aircraft, or always smashed the distributor in every vehicle they attacked, then critical supply chain shortages would be created, out of all proportion to the disabling effort required.[47]

In SOE's *Group B's Sabotage Handbook*, written by Blackden, there was also the recommendation that Brickendonbury's 'graduates' should encourage factory workers to adopt indirect 'go slow' methods.

> Whilst the effects of a 'Go Slow' policy in industry can be extremely important and should be practised wherever possible, results are bound to be limited by the operation of the piecework method of payment now of almost universal application. Ca'canny [Scottish term for a deliberate reduction of working speed and production] methods have been used from time immemorial in trade disputes, and it would be useless to attempt to detail them in this Handbook

as each worker and official will know the best way to apply them to his particular job. Organisers would, however, do well to cultivate non-collaborating managements, as where both management and workers are in collusion results will be many times greater. The drafting of workers to Germany offers a good approach to managements who may be prepared to remove skilled men to semi-skilled work in order to retain their services. Nevertheless the results obtainable by ca'canny methods are limited so that it is necessary to take more direct forms of attack.[48]

The handbook went on emphasise that incendiarism was a doubly attractive method for saboteurs. The damaging effects of using fire and water separately or in conjunction were highlighted. Potential saboteurs were told that the generous use of water in extinguishing a fire could cause damage out of all proportion to the size of the fire. Setting fire to a combustible building or its stock would result in a quantity of valuable machinery being exposed to the weather as well as fire hoses, resulting in delay, damage and disorganisation. It would also make it particularly difficult for the investigators to determine the cause of the fire.[49]

GENERAL PRINCIPLES OF ATTACK

In planning attacks upon industrial plant the following general principles should always be followed in order that the maximum value may be obtained for the effort put into that operation:-
a Attack cast iron in preference to steel – it is easier to damage and more difficult to repair.
b Attack machinery in motion rather than at rest, preferably at a bearing or main casting – the machine will then assist in its own destruction.
c Attack non-standard machines – they are less likely to be readily replaceable.
d Attack large complicated pieces, if possible in inaccessible situations – replacement and restoration is more difficult.

e On large-scale operations against similar targets, attack identical parts in each unit – this prevents the enemy from making one good machine out of several damaged ones.

f Always consider the possibility of achieving the object by means of fire, water, or smashing – explosives and manufactured stores are thereby rendered unnecessary and greater security is obtained.

g Always look for the bottleneck machines – production can often be stopped entirely if two or three vital machines are rendered useless.

Notwithstanding the above, the incidence of war-time conditions has had the effect of creating severe shortages of the most common types of machinery. The destruction or damaging of such items as motors, gear-boxes, pumps, etc., on auxiliary services is therefore likely to yield useful dividends under these circumstances and should not be overlooked.[50]

Another topic taught was blackmail sabotage, threatening owners of an industrial concern that if they did not agree to have selected parts of their works sabotaged, the RAF would be instructed to destroy it in air-raid bombing.

Towards the end of the war 'counter-scorching' was added to the curriculum. This was preventing the retreating enemy forces from actively sabotaging the very targets Brickendonbury students had been instructed to destroy. One imagines saboteurs gave advice to relevant staff at iron and steel works, engineering works and other factories and on the railways, airfields and ports on protecting their vital machinery and equipment.[51]

Ryder estimated that, by the time war ended in 1945, about 1,200 men had passed through Brickendonbury's various courses but made no mention of women. Its busiest period was between 1943 and 1944 when about thirty-five students a week were attending courses. It was a very cosmopolitan school with students from most Allied countries being trained there. Interpreters for each nationality had to be provided, which must have been a challenge as most students had had no experience in industrial work. Fundamental safety rules were laid down.

The SOE had a policy of sending its officers from its country sections on all their courses so that they had a better understanding of the work of the agents they were sending into the field. For example, Lieutenant Colonel Ronald Thornley, the head of X Section, Germany, scored the highest marks on his training course at Brickendonbury.[52]

Where Rheam was transferred to is not known. Blackden, who was appointed Chief Instructor in May 1943, was granted an emergency commission in the Royal Electrical and Mechanical Engineers, first as Captain and four months later as Major. When Brickendonbury closed he was sent to SOE Headquarters to finish writing the Industrial Sabotage Handbook and was then sent to Milton Hall, Peterborough (ME 65), as officer in charge of industrial sabotage to the Jedburgh agents destined for Europe and the Far East.[53]

CHAPTER 4

Early Sabotage Missions by Brickendonbury 'Graduates', 1940–1

Details of sabotage missions undertaken by agents trained by the SIS have yet to come to light. Their records, if they exist, are not as yet available for public scrutiny. According to Philby, two of their students had died. A Norwegian wireless operator was captured by the Germans and shot shortly after being dropped in Norway and a Belgian caught his parachute on the undercarriage of a plane and was flung to his death. The Spaniards were transferred to Beaulieu. The only sabotage Philby identified was an attack on the Iron Gates on the River Danube in an attempt to interrupt the supply of Romanian oil to the Germans. Section D did not have the resources in 1940 to do the job properly. The Yugoslav police discovered the plot and 'nipped it in the bud', causing considerable embarrassment to the British Government.[1]

It is possible that Alfred Rickman attended the Brickendonbury course. Rosander explains that, on 19 April 1940, his SIS-inspired attempt to halt iron-ore exports from Sweden to Germany was thwarted. Having recruited fellow saboteurs, reconnoitred the loading equipment at Oxelösund harbour and been given the go-ahead by Grand, he was betrayed to the Swedish police. A search of his house found 53.6 kg of explosives, fuses and detonators, said to have come from the British Embassy. A further 53.7 kg of explosives were found in his office and a cellar with eight landmines and 320 magnesium incendiary bombs. He spent four years in prison before returning to Britain.

There were plans to attack the Baku oilfields in the Caucasus but Grand did not have the men or the support needed to undertake them. According to Philby,

> In the field he [Grand] had little more than bits and scraps. His efforts to get more of the secret cake were frowned on by the older and more firmly based intelligence-gathering side of the service. Starting from the valid premise that sabotage and subversion are inherently insecure (the authors of 'bangs' are liable to detection), the intelligence people rushed happily to the invalid conclusion that bangs were a waste of time and money, diverting resources from the silent spy. Thus Grand's demands on the Treasury and on the armed services were often blocked within the service. At best they were given lukewarm support.[2]

The only people Philby saw as being prepared to offer resistance to Hitler after the Germans had taken over their countries were the Left-Wing parties, the peasant parties, the Social Democrats and the communists.

> Yet they were unlikely to stir for the sake of a British Government which insisted on playing footsie with the King Carols and Prince Pauls who had systematically persecuted them between the wars. Thus the ideologies of subversion in Britain started out under a heavy handicap imposed by the Foreign Office which failed to see until much too late, that, whatever the outcome of the war, the sun of its favourite puppets had set forever. Small wonder that, when the crunch came, the resistance movements leaned heavily towards the Soviet Union, and that the balance was only restored in France, Italy and Greece by a massive Anglo-American presence.[3]

SOE records, or more accurately those that were not destroyed in a fire after the war, are to be found in the National Archives in Kew.

Those considered sensitive were 'closed'. You may have heard of the Government's 'Thirty Year Rule', 'Fifty Year Rule' or 'Hundred Year Rule'. These kept documents out of the public domain either because they contained details of people still alive or the government did not want politically sensitive information disclosed. Every New Year the press report details from those documents that are 'opened'. However, with the Freedom of Information Act 2000, access to closed files has become much easier. For personnel files, the enquirer needs to provide evidence that the individual has reached the age of a hundred, a death certificate or an obituary.

Over the years since the Second World War, newspaper reporters and historians interviewed the men and women who were involved in wartime secret operations. Despite having signed the Official Secrets Act, some told their stories. Many, however, refused and kept their experiences a secret from their families and friends all their lives. Initially, the War Office vetted such publications and sensitive details were redacted, blanked out or removed and the names of individuals and places changed or deleted. Some people, probably having read their colleagues' accounts, felt prompted to write their memoirs. Enticed by a publisher, a number had their autobiographies published. Some had radio interviews and a number had television documentaries made on their exploits.

Over time, sensitivities about published accounts of espionage and clandestine activities diminished so that today, in the search for the truth of what happened during the Second World War, one can read numerous academic articles, military history books, web pages and even novels about these secret operations. Even films have been made about them and some students can now study the SOE for their GCSE.

Searching for details about Brickendonbury's graduates was not as daunting as I had expected. What follows are accounts of selected sabotage operations. Some, where there was more documentation available, are a lot more detailed than others. What has been noticeable though is that most accounts pay little if any tribute to Brickendonbury. This book hopefully acknowledges the role the school played in changing the fortunes of the Second World War.

In an SOE pamphlet entitled *Training Lectures & Statistics*, undoubtedly put together by training instructors, there were notes for organisers on all aspects of their work. One section in particular was of special interest for sabotage and is worth including in full.

TARGETS

Definition of the term 'target'. Anything attackable which is owned, controlled or helpful to the enemy's moral, physical or economic needs.

Organisers and agents must make a mental survey of possible targets in their area, not only for immediate purposes of attack, but also for future ones.

The relative value of the various targets should be carefully weighed. Consideration should be given to:

(a) How far will a successful attack affect the enemy?

(b) How far will a successful attack affect the local population in occupied territory?

(c) Can a planned attack be coordinated with other possible attacks, thereby increasing the effect of each and the enemy's general discomfort?

Notes:

(a) Where local population is inclined to complacently tolerate the enemy, it may be advisable to delay action until public opinion swings the other way.

(b) Reprisal. The enemy's favourite reply to subversive action. The community is penalised. The civilian population is as much in the front line as the fighting soldier. Every soldier trained in machine gun fire, knows that in an attack, he will have to cover his own side, with a barrage of fire aimed at the enemy's lines. This he *knows* will inflict casualties on his own compatriots. This knowledge does not stop him from putting down an effective barrage. He knows that by doing so he will prevent the enemy from inflicting higher casualties. This should serve as an analogy to those who have to weigh the pros and cons of reprisals.

(c) A coordinated plan of attack will be immensely more effective than haphazard operations. But do not put off a steady hammering at the enemy on every possible occasion. Keep your men busy and the enemy unhappy and constantly surprised.

4. Selection of Target
New organisers should, to start with, concentrate on small (or easy) targets. Ones not requiring elaborate preparation or more than one or two collaborators.

Remember, a target (however small) successfully attacked will inspire confidence in yourself and in your colleagues. More than that, a successful attack is like to fire the imagination of those not in the organisation. Dozens will spring up here and there to have an 'amateur' go at the enemy. The more the better!

5. Before Attack
(a) Each target should be carefully surveyed, line of approach studied; what protective measures guard the target (e.g. guards, alarm signals, locks on doors of buildings, barbed wire, etc.) means of approach:
  (i) By day
  (ii) By night.
(b) Possibilities of using bad weather as an ally.
(c) Possibilities of using the moon as an ally
(d) Possibilities of using national holidays as an ally.

6. Indirect Means of Attack
Example:
a Aeroplane factory is heavily guarded by day and night, and well fenced off by wire. Output important to enemy.

Survey shows that the instruments for the planes finished at this particular factory, are made in a small workshop in another part of the town; workshop practically unguarded.

Action: Destroy workshop; leave main factory alone. Until better able to attack it.
b Manufacturing town derives its power from a grid. Survey shows

that certain transformers are unguarded and stand well out of the town.

Action: Destroy transformers.

c Hydroelectric plant; survey shows power is derived from water brought by pipelines, five miles from plant.

Action: Destroy pipeline in mountain.

d Important telephone or telegraphic exchange is well guarded.

Action: Attack target outside the town by destroying overhead wires, poles or cables.

7. Attack

Necessity for every person connected with it to know:

(a) General plan.

(b) Place, date and time of assembly.

(c) The rendezvous.

(d) Each man's and woman's particular part.

(e) Each person's individual responsibility for bringing up tools and other necessities.

8. Leader

Attackers must obey leader and accept his decisions.

9. Getaway

A thorough reconnaissance before every attack should be made for the best possibilities of a quick get-away. As detailed a plan as possible for this purpose should be communicated to the attackers. This gives them a sense of confidence.

Remember that every attacker who gets away from a successfully 'put up' target, is worth double his weight again.

Remember that if attackers are caught, they may jeopardise the future of your organisations.

10. Never be outwardly jubilant about a victory, or celebrate one. It may make suspicious minds think. Go about your daily work quite unconcernedly. And don't worry; a time for celebration will surely come.

'OUR BUSINESS'

1. In our business, Improvisation must be resorted to. Apart from security, there are no rules.

2. You are unlikely to get ideal conditions for putting up any target. There's a snag somewhere. By improvisation, nine times out of ten the snag can be removed.

3. You have seen the various 'sweets' and 'toys' [explosives and detonators] that are at our disposal. They are good. Many new excellent gadgets are now in preparation. Some still in the experimental stage; some ready for market.

4. The best 'sweets and toys' are useless unless you have the men ready and eager to use them and will do so ruthlessly.

5. 'Sweets and toys' are only aids to our business. Natural elements are our main assets.

Natural Elements?

(a) Fire

(b) Water

(c) Wind and Draughts

(d) Sand

1. With these elements and improvisation you can do as much harm as with the best 'sweets and toys'.

2. Do not forget that great use can be made of iron filings and artificial wear and tear of machinery and running parts.

3. The broad Principles of '*Our Business*'.

(a) Get at the enemy's vitals, e.g. industry, war production, food.

(b) Get at his transport, rail, road, river; and at sea-going ports.

(c) Get at his communications: telegraph, telephone, wireless stations and postal services.

4. In 'Our Business' a job is a *good one*, if it looks like an accident, act of God or has 'no explanation'. It is bad if it stinks of being a deliberate crime with clues left all over the place.

5. Selection of Targets

Targets should be selected that they harass the enemy simultaneously in various parts of the territory under his control, and *undermine* his confidence and morale. The wider the distribution of targets, the greater the strain on his counter-espionage and anti-sabotage organisation, and thus the chances of detection are reduced.

6. Dream of promoting major disasters for the enemy; while planning them, cause as much minor inconvenience to him as possible by:

(a) Petty sets of damage.

(b) Tyre damage to cars.

(c) Derailment of trains.

(d) Damage to canal locks and gates.

(e) Sinking of barges in rivers and in docks.

(f) Destruction of telegraph wires.

(g) Burning anything that will naturally be apt to catch fire.

Remember, that men and women on hazardous operations work better if given some food before action. It may take hours under cover of darkness to get to a rendezvous. Sandwiches and a cup of coffee will hearten the operatives for their task.

7. Use of Women

(a) Women can be very clever and natural go-betweens especially if told sufficient to intrigue them. Generally speaking, they are loyal.

(b) Use women in 'Our Business' impersonally; sentimental angle always ends in difficulties.

(c) There is a danger that women may come under the influence of those whom they contact; if this is allowed for, the danger is minimised.

1. Future Possibilities

(a) Make continual contacts with people; you may not want them at the time; in future they may be invaluable.

(b) Keep a tab on likely people's hobbies, strong points, weaknesses.

1. Flexibility

Be ready and teach your agents to be ready to scrap plans that have perhaps taken months to prepare. If it is in the interest of 'Our Business' to do so.

1. General
Remember, and impress on agents that those working in the 'Un-uniformed' army, can be of the greatest assistance to the fighting forces and *will* affect the fortunes of their country.[4]

The earliest evidence of a Brickendonbury-inspired sabotage mission that has come to light so far was mentioned in Robert Fisk's article in the *Belfast Telegraph* about U-Boats in Eire. He tells the story of a man who asked to remain anonymous and who claimed that he trained at Brickendonbury and went on to become an expert in demolition, sabotage and bomb disposal. In 1940, as a lieutenant in the Royal Navy, he was sent to a base unit at HMS *Ferret* in Derry with five Royal Marines. Their mission was to 'prepare and supply equipment', incendiary and explosive charges, for fifteen marines and two officers aboard the Royal Fleet Auxiliary Tugboat *Tamara*. Commanded by Lieutenant Commander W. R. 'Tiny' Fell, who went on to design midget submarines, it was disguised as a trawler and had been searching unsuccessfully for German U-boats off the west coast of Ireland.

On 12 September 1940, he reported loading explosives on the *Tamara*, replacing them eleven days later when the boat returned to Derry. Fell was reported to have been blowing up fuel tanks in Cork that were thought to be being used to supply U-boats. Newly released British Cabinet papers suggest U-boat sightings in 1939 west of the Blasket Islands and near Bundoran, County Donegal, but there was no evidence of refuelling bases. Fisk was told that Germans were seen wearing uniforms, drinking in pubs, presumably coming ashore for unofficial R and R (Rest and Recreation) and to obtain provisions as Eire was neutral. While these reports could 'neither be accepted, nor wholly discounted', Fisk suggested that

many of the suppositions about German forces in the Irish Republic could be put down to the very German-looking uniforms used by the Irish at the time but which were changed in the 1940s ... Norwegian Allied troops also used German-style helmets in 1940 – often prompting patriotic Englishmen to arrest them.[5]

Following the German invasion of France in May 1940, Leslie
Humphreys, Section D's representative in Paris, escaped in a warship
from Bordeaux and was immediately ordered by the SIS to organise
a section that would send agents back. He had been liaising with
Rivet, the head of the Service de Renseignements, and Brochu, the
head of the French Cinquième Bureau, in developing clandestine
routes into Germany and sabotaging the German war effort. Within
a month, SOE had taken over Section D and he was appointed head
of F Section. Brochu, the head of the French Cinquième Bureau, sent
him a liaison officer and with his help, they recruited two dozen
volunteers from among the French refugees willing to be trained at
Brickendonbury.

Humphreys believed that the essential basis of all clandestine work
was good communication. His plan was to continue his efforts behind
enemy lines but, as the Norwegian, Danish, Dutch, Belgian and French
airfields and seaports were under German control, the only way to
infiltrate Allied agents was either by boat or submarine onto remote
beaches or by plane into isolated clearings away from any built-up
areas.

While this was possible early in the war, it became increasingly
difficult once the German Todt Corporation completed the
construction of the Atlantic Wall. This was a series of concrete
defensive gun emplacements along the coast from the southwest of
France to Norway. Consequently, the only way to help the various
resistance groups across Occupied Europe was clandestine night-time
drops into isolated fields.

To do this, in August 1940 the Air Ministry allocated the job to
No. 419 Flight, based at North Weald, about 20 miles north-east of
London between Harlow and Chelmsford in Essex. Using the short
take-off and landing Westland Lysanders, which were designed to
carry two passengers, they started infiltrating agents into France and
bringing people back. The SOE had taken over from the War Office
the responsibility of infiltrating Poles who were standing by, ready
to be dropped in to the Secret Army, but they were only allocated a
few Whitley bombers which were being used to parachute men into

Czechoslovakia and Poland. However, as the return flight to Warsaw took fourteen hours, their flights were limited to the moon periods during autumn and winter. Returning in daylight made the planes more susceptible to Luftwaffe attacks.

Frank Nelson, the head of SOE in 1940, was sent a paper in August 1940 arguing that one of their main tasks would be 'to recruit a carefully selected group of saboteurs who would operate exclusively against objectives on, or near, the coasts, at widely spaced points and at short notice. By March 1941, as the Special Duties Squadrons had undertaken two missions, one of Brittany and one to Poland, Gubbins, the Director of SOE's Training and Operations Section, was expressing the view that 'all the parties of men we are now training ... may well have to be landed by sea as no other means exist'.[6] By August the renamed 1419 Squadron had landed twenty-five agents and picked up five, whereas the Royal Navy had infiltrated nine by boat and submarine.

Brook Richards's research into the naval infiltration of SIS and SOE agents detailed the earliest attempts. Merlin Minshall worked for Ian Fleming in the Royal Navy's Naval Intelligence Division, which in late 1940 planned a joint mission with the SOE, code-named Operation Shamrock. He picked six of the French saboteurs at Brickendonbury, including Marcel Clech, Jean Pillet and a Monsieur Bernard. His plan was to be taken by submarine into the Bay of Biscay to capture a French fishing boat and use it to undertake reconnaisance about German U-boats that had begun operating from Brest, Lorient and La Pallice, French Atlantic ports, and investigate ways of sabotaging them before or after leaving port.

On 16 November 1940, they were taken to Greenock docks, near Glasgow, where they boarded HMS *Talisman*. A few days later they attacked a German tanker off Lorient but one of the torpedoes hit the seabed before it exploded. Avoiding the depth charges dropped by the tanker, they escaped undamaged. Eventually, they spotted a sailing tunnyman a few miles to the west of Ile-de-Croix on its way to the Atlantic fishing grounds. Minshall and the submarine captain decided that would be a suitable target so they surfaced and commanded the

French captain to send half his crew to the submarine. Minshall and his six men then commandeered the boat, named *Le Clipper*, and sailed it back to Britain.[7]

Intelligence obtained from the French crew revealed that ten Italian submarines were being used as blockade runners, attacking Allied convoys in the Atlantic. The boat was then used to infiltrate other agents onto the French coast.

Another French ship commandeered for the same purpose was *Le Rhin*. One of its crew appears to have been the first woman to be sent to Brickendonbury. Madeleine Bayard had her story told in Edward Marriott's *Claude and Madeleine: A True Story of War, Espionage and Passion*. Born in Paris on 21 February 1911, she married a French rubber plantation owner and in 1932 moved to a life of colonial luxury in Vietnam. Following his murder and her rape during a workers' rebellion, she was rescued by Claude Peri, a French naval officer who was in Vietnam working for the Deuxième Bureau. They became inseparable and returned to Europe where, when war broke out, he was instructed to use captured British explosives to blow up British shipping.

In June 1940, appalled by Marshall Pétain's capitulation to the Germans, Peri commandeered *Le Rhin*, a French ship, at Marseille with fifty-six seamen, sailed it to Gibraltar with Madeleine on board and handed it over to the British. Among the passengers was Albert Guèrisse, a Belgian soldier who had escaped from a French prison and adopted the cover name Pat O'Leary.[8]

Claude insisted that Madeleine accompany him on further naval missions so she given officer training at Greenwich and given a commission as First Officer in the WRNS (Women's Royal Navy Service). During this time she was able to improve her English. Following her training, she was reunited with Claude at the Hotel Piccadilly in London, where he introduced her to Commander John Langley, an SIS officer, who showed them some of his small stock of new sabotage weapons, 50 pounds of explosives and some new time pencils.

As there were plans to send Claude back into French waters on sabotage missions, this meeting resulted in Madeleine being sent to Brickendonbury with the cover name of Madeleine Barclay. Accompanying her was 'Pat O'Leary' who had been recruited by the SOE and was destined to return to the south coast of France to build up an escape network for downed aircrews and escaped prisoners of war. After being taught industrial sabotage, unarmed combat and explosive concealment, they were sent to Aston House.

According to Marriott, her

> training focused on the use of plastic explosive – referred to by Langley as 'cyclonite', by others as 'PE'. Most days were spent in the quarry in plain clothes, rigging charges under rail tracks and blowing the rear axles off decommissioned armoured cars. Writing later, Langley drew a picture of an endless succession of dangerous, pleasingly Boy-Scoutish experiments: 'We soon knew exactly how much was needed to derail a train, to blow a sizeable hole in the side of a ship, to detonate an ammunition dump, to destroy a large electrical substation, to shatter the tracks of a tank, in brief to do a great deal of damage behind the enemy lines with not much more than what looked like half a pound of butter and a tiny pencil fuse.'[9]

Exactly what her and Claude's mission was is unknown. All they were told was that they would be involved in the 'disruption' of German lines of communication. They left Liverpool docks on 6 April 1941 in *Le Rhin*, renamed HMS *Fidelity*, with Pat O'Leary as Second Officer. During the voyage to drop off agents on the Mediterranean coast of France, she was said to have been seen with sabotage and weapons handbooks that she had been issued at Brickendonbury with 'instructions for devices that now seem almost comically James Bond-ish: incendiary cigarettes, exploding coal, edible paper, explosives hidden in logs, time bombs secreted in Chianti bottles'.

Over the next few years she was involved in a range of clandestine activities in and around the Mediterranean until she was drowned when the HMS *Fidelity* was sunk by a U-Boat attack on 30 December 1943 in the North Atlantic.

After Peters resigned, he returned to the Navy and was given command of HMS *Tynwald*, an anti-aircraft cruiser in the Far East. He returned to England in August 1941 to assume duties as a Special Operations and naval planner in Operation Torch, the Allied invasion of North Africa. In this capacity, he advised Winston Churchill, then Prime Minister, and the admirals of the British and American navies.

'Nobby' Clarke, his replacement, was involved in the planning for Operation Reservist, part of Operation Torch. This was an attempt to make an early-morning landing of Allied troops in Oran harbour in Algeria, about 280 miles east of Gibraltar, surprise the Vichy French and capture their ships and port facilities to prevent them from falling into German hands. The rest of the Torch operation involved subduing the coastal defences of North Africa, improving Allied positions in the Western Desert and defeating Hitler's Afrika Korps.

According to Sam McBride, Peter's great-nephew Frederick had a sabotage specialist on board his ship. In fact, he had more. In Mark Reardon's article, 'Death at the Hands of Friends: Oran', he mentions twelve British Special Boat Service operatives having six 'folbots', folding kayaks, and 'mobile mines' to destroy the inner and outer boom protecting the entrance to the harbour. One presumes they were trained by Clarke in their use at Brickendonbury. Three teams under the command of Captain Harold Holden-White went on the HMS *Walney*. The other three, under the command of Lieutenant E. J. Lunn, went on the *Hartland*.[10]

Flying American flags in the hope that the French would not attack, in the early hours of 8 November 1942 Peters commanded the 250-foot destroyer HMS *Walney* accompanied by the HMS *Hartland*, two boats carrying British Commandos, soldiers of the 6th US Armed Infantry Division and a small detachment of US Marines. The saboteurs were not needed as he succeeded in ramming through the double boom of logs, chains and coal barges and sailed the 1½ miles towards the jetty. It was not the surprise they expected. Spotted by searchlights, they came under constant fire from four onshore batteries, a light cruiser and several anchored destroyers.

Despite releasing smokescreens, both ships suffered numerous direct hits. Peters was the only officer on the bridge to survive but was wounded in the shoulder and blinded in one eye. His ship, on fire and disabled, reached the jetty before sinking with flying colours. He and thirteen surviving crew members made it to the shore and were arrested. The other ship, HMS *Hartland*, was blown up and sunk with the loss of half its crew. Of the 393 Allied troops on board the two ships, 183 died and 157 were wounded, including 113 dead from the Royal Navy and 86 wounded, five US Navy dead and seven wounded.[11]

All the survivors were captured and imprisoned but, two days later, they were all freed when the French garrison surrendered to the Americans. By that time the French had systematically destroyed the harbour facilities, meaning that Peter's operation had failed but the other Allied landings at Casablanca and Algiers succeeded. The *London Gazette* reported on 18 May 1943 that 'on being liberated from the gaol, he [Peters] was carried through the streets where the citizens hailed him with flowers'. In recognition of his bravery in what was called 'a suicide charge', Dwight D. Eisenhower awarded him the Distinguished Service Cross, a US decoration second only to the Medal of Honour. Their citation stated that

> Captain Peters distinguished himself by extraordinary heroism against an armed enemy during the attack on that post. He remained on the bridge in command of his ship in spite of the fact that the protective armor thereon had been blown away by enemy shell fire and was thereby exposed personally to the withering cross fire from shore defenses. He accomplished the berthing of his ship, then went to the forward deck and assisted by one officer secured the forward mooring lines. He then with utter disregard of his own personal safety went to the quarter-deck and assisted in securing the aft mooring lines so that the troops on board could disembark. At that time the engine room was in flames and very shortly thereafter exploded and the ship turned on its side and sank.[12]

Research by McBride detailed how, on 13 November, three days after his release, he was flown back to England in a Sunderland seaplane, which encountered lightning, hail, sleet and 40-knot headwinds and then dense fog as it approached Plymouth Sound. Instrument failure resulted in the plane hitting the water, flipping over and splitting apart around a mile and a half from the entrance to the Devonport Dockyard near Plymouth. Miraculously, the eleven Canadian crew members survived. The four other passengers were killed in the crash or died from exposure in the water but Flight Lieutenant Wynton Thorpe, the pilot, found Peters still alive 'and valiantly tried to drag him to safety as he swam to a breakwater, giving up in exhaustion after about an hour when it was obvious that Peters was dead. A rescue boat from shore arrived about half an hour later to pick up survivors.'[13]

The British government posthumously awarded Peters the Victoria Cross. With no known grave, his body is thought to have sunk in Plymouth Sound. He is commemorated on the Portsmouth Naval Memorial, and Mount Peters, near Nelson in British Columbia, was named in his memory in 1946.

From October 1941 until the end of the war in June 1945 Brickendonbury was commanded by Lieutenant Colonel George Rheam, reckoned by Michael Foot, the military historian, to be 'the founder of modern industrial sabotage'. He was an exacting teacher, with the gift to foresee the sorts of problem his pupils were likely to encounter on the ground. Anyone trained by him could look over a factory with quite new eyes, spot the few essential machines in it and understand how to stop them with a few well-placed ounces of explosive; to stop them, moreover, in such a way that some of them could not be restarted properly by removing undamaged parts from comparable machines nearby.[14]

Groups of up to thirty-five students of all nationalities were given a four-week course before being flown out from Tempsford and other SOE airfields. Other targets attacked by them or members of the Resistance included airfields, airports, grounded aircraft, trains carrying troops and military supplies, naval and commercial shipping, berthed submarines, food and oil supplies, railway tracks, turntables, marshalling wards, railway sheds, railway repair depots, signals, road, rail and canal bridges, canals, lock gates, docks, warehouses, tank farms, prisons and even the Gestapo HQs in Copenhagen and Warsaw.

Research by Waldemar Grabowski has revealed that seventy-four Poles were sent to Brickendonbury. In November 1942 a young officer was stationed there as an instructor on Continental railways.[15] Details of the Poles' sabotage missions have yet to be uncovered.

CHAPTER 5

Brickendonbury and Operation Anthropoid: The Assassination of Reinhard Heydrich, Prague, Czechoslovakia, 1942

Two Czechoslovakians, Josef Gabčík and Jan Kubiš, were also trained at Brickendonbury for Operation Anthropoid. Their exploits have been published widely but few mentioned the preparation for their mission. On 20 October 1941, they were sent to Brickendonbury to learn specialised tactics in handling explosives. They were taught how to create improvised explosive devices and sabotage techniques on railroad tracks, bridges and houses. They were trained in the use of electric and chemical fuses by Captain Pritchard, a British explosives expert, who also taught them how to handle the specially designed grenades and sensitive time pencils.

Cyril Heath, a reporter for the *Herts and Essex Observer*, detailed part of their training:

> It was midnight. A fitful moon dodged in and out of scudding clouds, and in the distance an owl hooted dolefully. A long tree-lined driveway led to a big country house, and 23 men bent on revenge crouched for cover behind the bushes on either side of the road.
>
> Suddenly, in the distance, a car engine could be heard, and as it came closer, the men fidgeted, peering towards the main gates.
>
> The car swept up at speed; the men jumped out and attacked it, and then melted anonymously into the night.

A voice called them together. 'Congratulations, the attack was a complete success.'

The house was Brickendonbury, on the outskirts of Hertford; the year 1942, and the 23 men were Czechs, planning revenge on Reinhard Heydrich, German Reichsprotektor for Bohemia and Moravia ... The driveway at Brickendonbury was chosen for a rehearsal for the assassination of Heydrich, because it resembled the driveway of the house he was using as his headquarters.[1]

They were also sent to Aston House, where they practiced throwing Clarke's newly invented blast grenade on a slow-moving Austin. After completing their training and receiving the necessary false documents required to move safely through Czechoslovakia, Gabčík and Kubiš signed a pledge on 1 December 1941 in London, which stated,

The substance of my mission basically is that I will be sent back to my homeland, with another member of the Czechoslovak Army, in order to commit an act of sabotage or terrorism at a place and in a situation depending on our findings at the given site and under the given circumstances. I will do so effectively so as to generate the sought-after response not only in the home country but also abroad. I will do it to the extent of my best knowledge and conscience so that I can successfully fulfil this mission for which I have volunteered.[2]

Having signed their last will and testament, on 28 December, they boarded a Handley-Page Halifax at RAF Tangmere in Sussex and were parachuted, with several other agents, to a drop zone near Nehvizdy, a village close to Celakovice just east of Prague. Code-named Anthropoid, they had been equipped with two pistols, a 38 Colt – with four full spare magazines and 100 bullets – six armour-piercing bombs filled with plastic explosives, two magazines of fuses, two model Mills grenades, one Tree Spigot bomb launcher with one bomb, four electric fuses, one Sten Mk II machine gun with 100 bullets, 32 lbs of plastic explosives, 2 yards of fuse rope, four smoke bombs, a reel of steel string and three time pencils.

They made their way to Pilsen to rendezvous with other members of the Resistance and from there made their way to Prague, where they reconnoitred the area to choose the best place to assassinate Reinhard Heydrich, acting Reichsprotektor of Bohemia and Moravia. He was the former deputy to Heinrich Himmler, Obergruppenführer of the SS and destined to move to Vichy France. With the aim of using Czech labour to increase arms production and prepare the way for the ultimate Germanisation of Czechoslovakia, Heydrich's men had penetrated and virtually destroyed the Czech Resistance. Two Czech generals had been executed and many political figures were imprisoned. During the draconian measures he introduced in the first few months in power, 5,000 people were sent to concentration camps. To many he was known as the 'Beast', 'Butcher' or 'Hangman of Prague'.

They abandoned their initial plan to blow up the train on which Heydrich travelled in favour of blowing him up in the Mercedes he used to get to work. Russell Miller's research shows that they did not follow instructions to the letter. They had been instructed to gain

as much information as possible about HEYDRICH's movements in the first place, and then to get jobs as road sweepers. On the day chosen for the operation they were to begin sweeping the road at a selected corner. Their explosives and arms were to be concealed in their dustman's barrow and were to consist of three one-pound contact fused bombs, one four-second Mills bomb, one Colt Super 38 automatic pistol, to be carried by No. 1, and one one-pound contact fused bomb, one Colt Super 38 automatic pistol and one Sten gun (optional) to be carried by No. 2.

The first bomb was to be thrown by No. 1 at the front of the car when it came within 15 yards in order to kill the driver and so force the car to stop. The second bomb was then to be thrown broadside to hit the rear window, the panel just behind it or the rear door. Simultaneously No. 2 would open up with the Sten gun (or with his pistol if he had not been able to conceal the Sten gun under his coat). The Mills bomb was to be thrown into the car by No. 1 if HEYDRICH was not already dead, as contact bombs cannot be relied upon to explode if they hit soft surfaces.

The last contact bomb was to be retained by No. 2 as a reserve in case of failure of the primary attack. If a hit was not scored, the party was to kill HEYDRICH at close quarters with their Colt Super 38 automatic pistols, which they would carry in shoulder holsters.

In the event of the operation being successful the Colt pistols and spare bombs were to be used during the withdrawal, which was to be made separately.

A suitcase containing 30-lbs of Plastic Explosive was also to be concealed in the dustman's barrow. This suitcase would be fitted with a five-second delay fuse and could be thrown bodily at the car or, as a last resort, No. 1 was to rush the car with the suitcase in his hand while No. 2 threw his last bomb at the front axle.

At the request of the party themselves the operation was planned so that no attempt at withdrawal should be made or considered until HEYDRICH had been successfully liquidated, and they made it quite clear that, unless the initial action was entirely successful, both members of the party would share HEYDRICH's death.[3]

The Sten gun meant to riddle Heydrich's body jammed at the last minute as his car slowed down to turn the corner. The first of the two hand grenades thrown at the car exploded, but only wounded him. Heydrich managed to get out of the car, draw his pistol and shoot back at the assassins before collapsing in the street. The chauffeur gave chase but was shot with the SOE trademark, two rapid gunshots. The two assassins got away on bikes and claimed sanctuary in St Cyril and Methodius church. Heydrich was rushed to hospital and, with blood transfusions, survived for eight days. He died on 4 June from blood poisoning brought on by fragments of auto upholstery, steel and his own uniform that had lodged in his spleen.

German retaliation was swift and ruthless. Curfews were put in place, thousands arrested and almost 200 men were killed at Lidice, where the Germans thought the assassins had safe houses. About 200 women were sent to concentration camps where most died. Eighty-seven children were sent to concentration camps at Gneisenau and Chemnitz and gassed, and those who looked German were sent to a Nazi orphanage. The buildings were dynamited one by one and bulldozers and ploughs brought in to level the site completely until not a trace remained. The whole event was captured on five hours of film. A grain crop was planted over the flattened soil and the name was then removed from all German maps. When news leaked out it shocked the world.

At 0400 hours on 18 June, 800 Gestapo troops surrounded the church of St Cyril and Methodius in Prague, broke in and, after a two-hour battle, shot dead two of the agents in the choir loft. One was fatally wounded and, unable to shoot himself, was taken to hospital but died on arrival. A long assault on the crypt took place with tear gas and water hoses used. After many hours, to avoid capture, the other four turned their guns on themselves.

The following day, General Elias, the imprisoned former Premier, was executed. The two Serb bishops who had provided sanctuary were sentenced to death and publicly hanged. 263 Czechs were said to have been arrested, including 222 of the agents' relatives and nine members of the Cathedral administration, and shot at Mauthausen concentration camp, with the women and children gassed. Five days later, on learning that the attackers had used a wireless set in the village of Lezaky, the Nazis killed thirty-two villagers, deported eleven to concentration camps and razed the eight stonecutters' shops and poor villagers' cottages to the ground.

Between May and September 1942, it is said that about 6,000 people were arrested and 3,000 murdered. All Czech Orthodox Christian churches were closed and their property confiscated. Although Gabčik and Kubiš's mission was successful, the German reprisals were thought to have exacted a very high price and the Czechoslovakian Resistance in Prague was damaged so much that it was only able to resume its activities at the very end of the war.[4]

CHAPTER 6

Brickendonbury and the Sabotage of the Heavy Water Plant at Vemork, Rjukan, Norway, 1942–4

Following Operation Weserübung, the German occupation of Norway, on 9 April 1940, their troops proceeded to take over important military and industrial sites across the country. After two months' desperate resistance, on 7 July King Kaakon VII, Crown Prince Olav, the Norwegian government and a number of military personnel fled to England with the British forces sent to help them. On 10 July, Norway surrendered. Those involved in the escape route across the North Sea using fishing boats and motorboats to reach the Shetland Isles were known as 'The Shetland Bus'. Motivated to fight Nazi oppression, some escaped from Sweden, aided by representatives of the SIS and SOE stationed in the British Embassy in Stockholm. Others got out via Russia, India, China, Canada and the United States.

Once in Britain, they were escorted either by train or boat to London where they spent several days being interviewed at the Royal Victoria Patriotic School in Wandsworth. British intelligence officers were not only keen to identify whether they were potential spies, they also wanted up-to-date information about conditions in Norway and any useful information about German troop and weapons installations. Another reason was to identify men willing to join the Norwegian Armed Forces in exile.

From its inception, the SOE had a Scandinavian section with headquarters at Chiltern Court on Baker Street. It was headed from August until December 1940 by Charles Hambro, a wealthy British banker who had relatives in Norway and who saw at first hand what Nazi occupation was like. He was keen to recruit potential agents from among the evacuees. One of those who escaped in April 1940 was thirty-nine-year-old Lieutenant James Chaworth-Musters, the British vice-consul and a Norwegian speaker. Known to his friends as Mouse, due to his academic interest in rodents, he was recruited into Section D's Scandinavian section. Martin Linge, one of Chaworth-Musters's neighbours and a close friend in Bergen, who had escaped with him, was also recruited and both were given the task of interviewing Norwegian escapees and identifying men willing to go back to Norway. In autumn 1940, after working as the Liaison Officer between the Section D and the Norwegian government-in-exile, Linge got involved with advising the new recruits being trained to return to Norway.

The first Norwegians sent to Brickendonbury for sabotage training were Ruben Langmo, who had been recruited by D Section, Gunnar Fougner, Nils Nordland, Odd Starheim, Frithjof Pedersen Kviljo and Alf Lindberg. The last three had bought fuel, pint-by-pint, until they had enough to drive a motorboat across the North Sea, arriving in Aberdeen on 17 August 1940.[1]

From December 1940, escaped Norwegian military personnel were based in requisitioned properties across Britain. Initially, they were accommodated at Brock Hall, near Flore, Northamptonshire. Some stayed at Stodham Park (STS 3), near Liss in Hampshire. As the numbers increased, they moved to Fawley Court (STS 54b), a much larger property with extensive grounds outside Henley-on-Thames, near London. Their paramilitary training was at Arisaig House (STS 21), Inverness-shire in north-west Scotland, with another base for mountain warfare and ski training at Drumintoul Lodge (STS 26a), Aviemore. Their parachute training, like other SOE-trained agents, was at Ringway aerodrome (STS 51), now Manchester airport. Training in clandestine warfare was at The Rings (STS 35), one of eleven requisitioned country houses, on Lord Montagu's estate at Beaulieu in the New Forest, Hampshire. Those destined for wireless training went to Thame Park (STS 52), near Oxford. Those needing more specialised training in ground-to-air wireless communication went to Howbury Hall (STS 40), near Bedford, and those who were to undertake sabotage work, went to Aston House (STS 12), near Stevenage, and Brickendonbury Manor (STS 17), near Hertford.

In Ray Mears's *The Real Heroes of Telemark*, he states that the Norwegians' 'demolition training was provided by explosives experts, engineers and architects, who taught the recruits the most effective and economical ways of destroying factories, houses, barracks, bridges, dams, trains, gates, reservoirs, port installations, railway lines and ships'.[2]

Once their training at Brickendonbury was finished, they were accommodated at Grendon Hall (STS 53a), one of SOE's 'holding stations', near Aylesbury, Buckinghamshire, until their flight was arranged. From April 1942, they were accommodated at Gaynes Hall (STS 61), near St Neots, about half an hour's drive from RAF Tempsford in Bedfordshire, from where most of their flights took off. In the early years of the war, converted Whitley bombers were used but later modified Halifax and Stirling bombers. To reach Norway, pilots had to fly north to the Naval Air Station at Kinloss on the north-east coast of Scotland, refuel and then cross the North Sea.

In March 1941, the SOE created the Norwegian Independent Company No. 1 and Linge was appointed Captain and put in charge. Its aim was to send trained men on commando raids back into Norway, to support and supply the various Norwegian resistance movements as well as to undertake sabotage missions. In January 1942, SOE divided the Scandinavian section into national sections and the Norwegian section was formed, headed by Lieutenant Colonel John 'Tug' Wilson, code-named SN, and Naval officer James Chaworth-Musters, code-named DG.

Ruben Langmo, a twenty-year-old military policeman, escaped from Norway in May 1940 by using the 'Shetland Bus' and, following his debrief, joined the Norwegian Independent Company No. 1, an elite group of well-trained Norwegians. He was sent to Brickendonbury and provided with detailed instructions in how to destroy the Bjølvefossen hydro-electric power station at Ålvik, about 40 miles east of Bergen. In 1905 the river flowing down the steep mountainside into the Hardanger Fjord had been piped to drive a turbine. The generator provided the power for a smelting works that produce ferrosilicon and silicon-based alloys, much needed in the German steel industry. Provided at Brickendonbury with detailed maps, aerial photographs, plans of the works and machinery, he was told exactly where to place the plastic explosives that were intended to destroy the plant.[3]

Details of the mission have yet to come to light. It appears to have been organised by D Section before the SOE was formed and their archive is not yet accessible to the general public. Langmo, with Kalle Kronberg as second-in-command, was dropped with eleven others from a fishing boat on 16 June 1940. The team blew up the pipeline, which put the plant out of commission for several months. This was the first of many sabotage operations against industrial targets in Norway.[4]

The German response to early acts of sabotage was evidenced in an anonymous report dated 1940 and headed 'Norway Sabotage':

> Dagens Nyheter, 24.11. German military property in the district of Bergen is being constantly sabotaged and damaged despite measures taken by the secret police. The damage is so comprehensive that the authorities in Bergen offer rewards of 1,000 N. Cr. for information leading to the discovery of the perpetrators of certain acts, and urge the population to inform the police, thus enabling them to bring the culprits to justice.[5]

One imagines that the SOE and the escaped Norwegians were aware of the consequences of being caught. The Brickendonbury instructors must have stressed the importance of planning their escape as a vital addition to their training.

Another of the early Norwegians trained at Brickendonbury was twenty-four-year-old Odd Starheim. On 1 January 1941, he was put ashore by a British submarine at Farsund, a remote harbour on the south-west coast of Norway between Stavanger and Kristiansand. Part of his mission was to set up a wireless transmitter so that messages could be sent back to the SOE in London and for messages to be received with instructions about supply drops and missions. By the end of the war, there were sixty-five wireless sets operating across Norway. It is very likely that another part of Starheim's mission was to make contact with Einar Skinnarland, a twenty-three-year-old Norwegian graduate from the Telemark Engineering College and engineer at the Møsvatn dam, as he reportedly fed reports about his company's operations to London. Norsk Hydro-Elektrisk, the Norwegian hydro-electric authority, had dammed the river from Hardangervidda where it flowed down from the steep-sided Vestfjord valley at Vemork on the Barren Mountain near Rjukan, about 50 miles west of Oslo. The water was piped down a 144-metre drop onto turbines that were capable of generating 60 megawatts of electricity. Attached to the power station was an electrolysis plant, which was built to manufacture chemical fertilisers, but Skinnarland told London that, from 1934, the plant had been used to manufacture 'heavy water', deuterium oxide (D_2O). His brother was the warden at Møsvatn dam so he was privy to vital information. Professor Leif Tronstad and his colleague, Doctor Jomar Brun, had managed to extract it from the residue water after electrolysis. In normal water it occurs in concentrations of 1:6,000. After electrolysis it was 1:2,300. The plant at Rjukan was the only industrial-scale facility in Europe with a capacity of producing 12 tonnes a year.

As Norsk Hydro had sold heavy water to both France and Germany before the war, following the German invasion of Norway, the Deuxième Bureau, the French military intelligence, with the assistance of the company's director, 'borrowed' 185 kg. Along with research papers, it was smuggled to Britain with the assistance of the British merchant navy. Where it was stored is unknown but one imagines that the government scientists were able to warn the War Office of its military potential.

In the American 'Manhattan Project', they were using heavy water as a coolant and moderator in their production of the atomic bomb.

Realising that if the Germans could secure supplies of heavy water to produce their own atomic weapons it would be a significant threat to the Allies, British physicist Reginald Jones, the head of the British Air Staff's scientific intelligence and scientific adviser to the SIS, recommended that action be undertaken to destroy the plant.

The intelligence Skinnarland had gathered included the structure and fortification of the Vemork works, where the guards were billeted, how many were on duty at any one time and where the sentries were on the suspension bridge between Vemork and Rjukan. Between 1940 and 1941 there had been a drought which had reduced river flow but, following the snow melt in the spring, the Germans were planning to order the company to step up production and transport the stockpiles of heavy water from Norway to Germany.

When thirty-eight-year-old Tronstad, a fervent patriot, was ordered by the Germans to supervise the rapid construction of new apparatus at the plant, he tried to slow it down by injecting small quantities of castor oil and cod liver oil into existing stocks.[6] By summer 1941, when the Germans began to suspect him, he received orders from London to come to England via Sweden. In his 'absence', Brun was appointed the new chief manager and became a vital source of intelligence for the Allies, sending microphotographs hidden in toothpaste tubes and handing documents to SOE agents who arranged for them to be taken to England via Sweden.

In September 1941, during his interrogation at the Royal Victoria Patriotic School, Tronstad revealed that he had been a professor of inorganic chemistry at the Norwegian Institute of Technology. As one of the pioneers of heavy water research and having been involved in the construction of the plant at Vemork, he was able to provide the British scientific, intelligence and military circles with valuable details.

Instead of being allowed to return to Norway on active service, the Norwegian High Command in England appointed Tronstad a Major and put him in charge of Section IV with special responsibility for operations against Norwegian industry and coastal shipping, training of commando units from the Norwegian Company No. 1 for operations in

Norway and technical guidance on sabotage. In this capacity he had to liaise with the SOE and the Norwegian government-in-exile. Tronstad was also involved with the specialised technical and demolition training at Brickendonbury.[7]

On 4 March 1941, Linge headed a party of fifty men as part of Operation Claymore. Whether they were prepared for the mission at Brickendonbury is uncertain. They were part of a larger attack of over 500 commandoes on the Lofoten Island, north-west Norway. He and his men successfully blew up fifteen fish-oil and glycerine factories and destroyed 3,600 tons of oil and glycerine. 18,000 tons of shipping were sunk in the naval attack and an armed German trawler, *Krebel*, was captured. While temporarily reducing the supply of raw material in the manufacture of nitroglycerine, on board the trawler were found a code book and a spare set of rotor wheels for the Enigma cypher machine, which enabled the decoders at Bletchley Park to read German naval codes. The returning British ships brought 315 Norwegian volunteers to Britain. Linge's men, acting as guides and interpreters, also arrested a number of Quislings, Norwegians who were collaborating with the Germans.[8]

A few days later, the SOE received a radio report informing them that, although the buildings had been largely destroyed, the plant was working again. This prompted them to start sending more men from Kompani Linge to Brickendonbury for training to attack larger-scale industrial complexes. On 2 January 1942, Odd Starheim and fellow agent Andreas Fasting were the first Norwegian agents to be dropped 'blind', without a reception committee, onto snow-covered ground in Norway. In Freddie Clark's *Agents by Moonlight*, he detailed how

P/O Smith, in his first operation as a Whitley captain flew CHEESE/ FASTING to Norway. The target was on the southernmost tip of Norway in the Flekkefjord area. Smith encountered trouble with his port airscrew soon after leaving the English coast at Cromer. He decided to continue and crossed the Norwegian coast 16 km south of Flekkefjord where there was 2/10th cloud and patches of mist.

However the target area was clear and they dropped two agents and
a package successfully from 2,000 feet. Three parachutes were seen to
open, two were camouflaged, one white.[9]

Using the wireless set that was dropped with them, they had to re-
establish radio contact with the SOE as the previous radio operator
had stopped transmitting. They also had instructions to meet up with
Skinnarland whose other messages had helped the Royal Navy sink the
Bismarck and cripple the *Prinz Eugen*. Skinnarland did not need a lot
of persuasion to come to England and help plan a sabotage mission on
the heavy water plant. In March 1942, Starheim, Skinnarland and four
other Norwegians hijacked the 600-ton coastal steamer *Galtesund*,
ordering the captain at pistol-point to change course to Aberdeen. An
urgent radio message ensured RAF air cover for a trip through atrocious
weather across the North Sea.

When Brun was similarly smuggled out of Norway and brought to
England with his wife, he provided the SOE with fresh intelligence
about the Vemork plant. Hambro was informed that the Germans
were producing about 2 tons of heavy water each year but were
planning to increase that to 4.6 tonnes. Plans were put in place to
destroy the plant. However, Tronstad put forward the argument of
Major General Hansteen, the Commander-in-Chief of the Norwegian
Armed Forces, that widespread damage to the plant would put it out
of action for years. Around 200 locals' livelihood depended on the
plant and, vital for Norway's agriculture as it was producing chemical
fertiliser, its destruction would affect the country's food production.
The hydro-electric plant was Norway's largest industrial enterprise
and destroying it completely would be a major blow to the country's
economy. It was on Tronstad's advice that a bombing mission to destroy
the Vemork plant was dismissed in favour of sabotage. He argued that
a night-time RAF bombing raid may not hit the target and any bombs
that did hit would probably destroy the ammonia chambers and kill
innocent civilians. Carefully placed charges of plastic explosive would
be a better plan and, to avoid reprisals against the local resistance, he
suggested that the saboteurs deliberately left behind items that would

indicate the attack had been undertaken by British, not Norwegian, agents. At a Cabinet meeting, it was immediately decided to send thirty specially trained sappers, engineer troops, to destroy the heavy water plant.

The Directorate of Combined Operations was given responsibility and SOE was given the task of selecting and training the men, arranging their air transport, getting them to Vemork, providing them with wireless communications and supplying the weapons, plastic explosives and other supplies needed for what was called Operation Freshman. The head of the newly formed Norwegian section, Lieutenant Colonel Wilson, would have been kept busy with phone calls, telegrams and memoranda pertaining to the operation. One plan put forward was to land the men by PBY Catalina, an American flying boat, on Lake Møsvatn, 15 miles from the plant. This was abandoned because the lake would be frozen and the mountains too steep for commandoes to climb. Instead it was decided that a raid by glider-borne troops would have the best chance of success.

The geographical problems to overcome for such an attack on the Vemork plant were considerable. While the mountains presented ideal territory for the Norwegian Resistance, access was often only by foot-tracks, accommodation would be in ski-huts on the saeters (high mountain pastures) and there would be no food supplies. Food had to be obtained from settlements in the valleys or be dropped by parachute, otherwise the men had to use the fieldcraft skills that they had been taught by the SOE to survive in the wild.

The weather was always uncertain and, being so close to the Arctic Circle, from May to September there was virtually no darkness. This made escape by sea virtually impossible as the boats would be easily spotted. As a result the 1,000-mile border with Sweden was the best escape route. Mountains were dangerous for parachute drops and the safest place was on frozen lakes. Also internal communication was worse for the guerrillas than for the locals as post and wireless transmissions were easily checked and the safest method was messages being taken by hand, running the gauntlet of German road controls. This explains why the Tempsford crews had to supply them with

'Eureka', a recently developed radio transmitter that, when switched on, sent out a signal, which the radio operator on board the overflying plane could pick up with their 'Rebecca' equipment. This allowed the pilot to fly directly to the point of transmission and locate the drop zone, usually termed DZ by those in the SOE. Later in the war, they were supplied with S-phones, an early mobile phone device which allowed an agent on the ground to communicate directly with a radio operator on a plane flying overhead.

Eleven days after Skinnarland's arrival in Scotland, he was given a twelve-day crash course in sabotage and coding. Very likely he spent some time at Brickendonbury. On 28 March, the day after a practice parachute jump from an air balloon at Ringway, he was flown out of Kinloss in Scotland in a Whitley bomber. Once the green light indicated he could jump, he froze. It was his first ever flight and he was petrified. It took twenty minutes to persuade him to jump, while the pilot circled the DZ. When he was told that the aircraft could not fly like that any longer, he was persuaded to jump. He landed safely on the snow-covered mountains near his home in Hardangervidda. Code-named 'Swallow Blue', Skinnarland used the latest wireless set dropped with him to contact London. Early sets weighed around 30 pounds but SOE's boffins managed to develop new sets before the end of the war that weighed only 14 pounds. When he got back to work he claimed that he had been ill, but had had a relaxing break. He stayed in Norway undetected until liberation, sending details about German troop positions around Rjukan and providing valuable communication for Operation Bittern.

After three flights had to be cancelled due to bad weather, the air liaison officer at Tempsford disregarded the request that the drop was not done on a Saturday night as people might be out walking in the DZ. It was the last chance during the September–October moon period. Maybe it was thought people would not be out and about in the early hours of a Sunday morning. At 2305 hours on 3 October 1942, Flight Lieutenant Sutton flew what Clark claimed was a team of four trained assassins who had been instructed 'to liquidate known denouncers' in Norway, 'brought about due to fears of the local population about reprisals'. Thor Helliessen, Johannes S. Andersen, Ruben Langmo and Jan Allen parachuted from 700 feet into Nordmakra, north of Oslo, with six containers and a list of sixty-two known denouncers. When they rendezvoused with representatives of Milorg, there were objections to the plan. Milorg was the underground Norwegian military organisation responsible for intelligence gathering, sabotage, supply missions, raids, espionage, transport of imported goods to rural areas, releasing Norwegian prisoners and escorting people fleeing overland to neutral Sweden. Worried that the Germans would find out about them, start making reprisals and increase their defences around the plant at Vemork, they persuaded the agents to provide them instead with weapons and sabotage training.

Given the long hours of daylight in Norway over the summer, any RAF flight would not be considered to have a reasonable chance of avoiding enemy flak until the autumn. This gave time for the engineers at Brickendonbury to build a large-scale replica of the Rjukan plant to familiarise agents with every nook and cranny of the place. Outbuildings were altered so that they closely resembled the target.

An advance party of four Norwegian agents – Jens Anton Poulsson, Arne Kjelstrup, Knut Haukelid and Claus Helberg – code-named Grouse, were taken to Brickendonbury for specialised training. When they visited and for how long they stayed have yet to come to light. The main party, thirty-four Royal Engineers from the 1st British Airborne Division, part of Mountbatten's Combined Operations Unit, were chosen for what was designated Operation Freshman and received arduous training in Wales and Scotland before being sent to Brickendonbury for specialised instructions. When they arrived and for how long they stayed is unknown.

After two flights were cancelled due to bad weather and technical difficulties, on 18 October Wing Commander Hockey of 138 Squadron piloted his Halifax on Grouse 2, parachuting four agents and eight containers onto a small mountain plateau at Fjarefit on the Hardangervidda, a remote wilderness in the Songedal area that was avoided by German troops. The Grouse team spent fifteen days trekking east to the Møsvatn area. Twenty-three-year-old Jens Poulsson, the commander of the operation, was forced to use his SOE-taught fieldcraft skills while he awaited the arrival of the Gunnerside team. In an interview held at the Imperial War Museum he said that

'Gunnerside' was supposed to join us in December, before Christmas, but the weather was very bad and they didn't arrive until the middle of February '43. In the meantime we had to fend for ourselves. To stay alive we needed wood and we needed food. Before Christmas we had a very bad time and we had to eat reindeer moss, or rather Icelandic moss. We mixed it with some oatmeal we had. It was only a few times we tried that. So we were dependent on hunting and the day before Christmas I shot the first reindeer. In all I think we shot fourteen reindeer, which was our main source of food. We used the contents of the stomach as a vegetable. The reindeer did the preliminary cooking for us so we just mixed it with blood and used it with the meat. We used everything from the animal, except the skin and the feet.[10]

Eventually, they made contact with Torstein, Skinnarland's brother. Having reconnoitred the area and located a suitable landing site for gliders that was unable to be seen by German patrols, 3 miles south-west of the dam, messages were sent back to London with advice on the best way to attack the plant.

Located in a steep-sided, forested valley below the 5,400-foot-high Gausatoppen mountain, the power station had been built on a broad rock shelf, about 1,000 feet above the fast-flowing river. The four men had to survive four months camped out in an eyrie above Hardanger plateau in freezing temperatures awaiting instructions. They learned that Generaloberst Nikolaus von Falkenhorst, the Commander-in-Chief of the German forces in Norway, had visited the plant and warned the staff that it could be a target of another attack. However, he did not have the manpower available to defend it sufficiently. London was informed that, during the summer, there were fifty-five soldiers guarding the plant and twenty guarding the dam, but during the winter there were only twelve at the plant, twelve at the dam and forty in Rjukan.

Most were either elderly or infirm Austrians commanded by an elderly captain, but occasionally well-trained German troops visited the area and Skinnarland learned that there were Gestapo agents operating in the area.

Three iron hawsers had been erected across the valley to bring down any low-flying British or American bombers and most of the defences were concentrated on the ridge above the plant. Minefields and booby traps defended the hillside above the plant as this was the route thought that a potential attack would come. There were searchlights on the roof and a machine gun placed near the entrance, and a single-span bridge, protected by two guards, led to the plant's entrance. As there were around 300,000 German troops in Norway at the time, some could easily reach the area to prevent a large force of attackers from escaping to Sweden.

As the SOE had established an intelligence network in Stockholm by late 1940, agents sent into Norway were provided with addresses and passwords for safe houses across Sweden. This organisation could provide shelter and safe passage back to England.

On 17 November, Grouse sent a message to London saying that the weather was not perfect but they considered that it had improved enough for a drop. Flights were immediately arranged from Tempsford to Scotland and, two days later, two Halifax bombers set off from Wick towing two Horsa gliders carrying the trained commandoes and their explosives. It was the first such glider operation of the Second World War. The 400-mile journey to Norway was the longest glider tow ever attempted at that date. Their mission was

> to destroy the stocks of 'Lurgan' [the code-name for heavy water], the importance of which far ascends all other objectives, and only after their destruction has been assured to carry out such demolitions as will deny to the enemy the productive capacity of the Norsk Hydro Works.[11]

Were any to be injured, they were to be issued with morphine and left behind.

A mechanical fault in the Rebecca unit in the first Halifax meant that the radio operator could not pick up the signal from the Grouse team's Eureka, which would have guided them to the DZ. In desperate weather conditions and far from the target, the telephone link between the glider and the plane broke. They crossed the coast at 10,000 feet but the navigator could not locate the DZ. Low on fuel, the pilot turned back but ran into such violent turbulence that the 300-foot towline broke. The glider crash-landed on the side of Lysefjord at Fyljesdal. Eight commandoes were killed, four were seriously injured and five escaped unhurt. Found by local farmers, they wanted help in escaping to Sweden. This was considered impossible. Their maps and other documents were burned before German Waffen SS and army troops arrived. The dead were buried in a shallow grave and the nine survivors were forced to walk to one of the boats. The pilot of the first Halifax managed to struggle back to base for a very awkward debrief.

The second Halifax failed to find Grouse's reception lights and continued to circle. The cloud level dropped and the plane began to ice up. As the pilot tried to gain height, the frozen tow rope broke and the plane crashed into the side of Hestadfjell mountain, 10 miles inland. Six aircrew and a number of commandoes were killed instantly. When the German authorities arrived on the scene, the dead bodies were thrown into a bog.

The glider spiralled out of control and crash-landed in the mountains between Bjerkreim and Helleland. Seven commandoes were killed instantly. Two survivors went to find help for the seriously wounded. The man they met told them that the nearest doctor was 15 kilometres away and, to contact him, he would need to use the telephone, which would mean the Germans operating the exchange would learn about them. Hoping that they would be treated as prisoners of war, the two men agreed. Before help arrived at the crash site, all the important documents were burned. The survivors were arrested and duly taken to the German camp at Slettebo, near Egersund.

Leo Marks, one of the SOE's code experts, commented in his wartime autobiography, *Between Silk and Cyanide*, that he was shocked when he read all the deciphered messages from Grouse and Stockholm describing atrocities carried out by the Quisling government and the Gestapo afterwards. The Germans were following Hitler's Commando Order issued on 18 October 1942, which stated that 'all terrorist and sabotage troops of the British and their accomplices who do not act like soldiers but rather like bandits will be treated as such by the German troops and will be ruthlessly eliminated in battle whenever they appear'.

Of the nine commandoes who survived the first glider's crash, five had their hands tied behind their backs with barbed wire. They were then taken to a concentration camp and tortured. Three of the injured were taken to a hospital in Stavanger where a Quisling doctor injected air bubbles into their veins causing instant death. The fourth was shot in the back of his head. All four bodies were dumped at sea. The five uninjured were held until 18 January 1943 and then taken to nearby woods and shot. The fourteen who survived the second crash were taken initially to Bekkebo barracks, then taken into the woods and shot one by one. Their bodies were buried in unmarked graves. Every man executed was in full uniform. It was claimed that the Germans found all the containers dropped for the operation with their weapons, ammunition, explosives, wireless equipment and maps. Norwegian citizens in the Hardanger area were punished. Homes were burnt, women and children arrested and hundreds of innocent people taken hostage and sent to concentration camps, but the Grouse team managed to evade capture.

After the war, the head of the Gestapo in Oslo, who had ordered the executions, committed suicide before the Allies liberated Norway. Several Wehrmacht officers implicated in the execution were tried. One was shot, another hanged and a third extradited to the Soviet Union for other war crimes. Von Falkenhorst was also found guilty of two of the Freshman deaths and sentenced to death but, on appeal, it was commuted to twenty years.

Although the operation was considered a failure, it demonstrated to the War Office the range, flexibility and possibilities of airborne forces and glider operations, as well as identifying equipment failures. These problems were resolved for Operation Market Garden, the Allied advance through Belgium towards Holland. The Rebecca-Eureka homing device system was improved so that the Mk II, when it was ready in 1943, was reported as having a 95 per cent success rate.

When Grouse informed London that production at Vemork had restarted and the Germans were stockpiling heavy water, another mission was organised, code-named Gunnerside. Twenty-three-year-old Lieutenant Joachim Rønneberg, a sabotage and demolitions instructor at the SOE's training camp at Aviemore in Scotland, was asked to choose a five-man team. He chose thirty-one-year-old Birger Strømsheim as his second-in-command for his coolness and maturity as a weapons instructor and his street-fighting skills. The others were thirty-two-year-old Knut Haukelid, twenty-four-year-old Fredrik Kayser, twenty-four-year-old Kasper Idland and twenty-seven-year-old Hans Storhaug. On 10 December 1942 the six-man team went to Brickendonbury to prepare for the attack. A note in Strømsheim's file stated that it was a short four-day course. In order to maintain the utmost secrecy, all the other 'students' were evacuated.

Under the supervision of Tronstad and Brun, the sabotage party were provided with an exact, up-to-date replica of the Vemork heavy water room. They practiced laying explosives on the imitation cylinders, including in the dark. All six were made to carry out the exercise over and over again until they could do it at great speed and without even having to think about it. In Mears's book he quoted Rønneberg:

'Jomar Brun had arrived in Britain bringing with him very detailed drawings of the plant and as a result of it I can confidently say that no sabotage operation launched from Britain into occupied Europe at this time enjoyed better information than ours ... I was even told where to find the key to the lavatory to lock up the Norwegian guard. None of us had been to the plant in our lives but by the time we left Britain we knew the layout of it as well as anyone.'

During the week the group were also given intense physical training as well as shooting practice with Colt. 325 and tommy guns. One evening during their training the six men were handed new firearms as they wound down at the end of another day. Five minutes later the sound of gunfire could be heard coming from the room and the instructor rushed in and saw a hole in the wall. 'What the hell is going on?' he snapped. To which Rønneberg replied calmly: 'We are just testing our new weapons and mine appears to work.'[12]

Before they left Brickendonbury, Tronstad told them,

'You have been told what happened to the airborne troops and you must reckon that in no circumstances will the Germans take any prisoners. For the sake of those who have gone before and who have died, I beg you to do your utmost to make the operation succeed. You know how important it is, and what you do now will be part of Norway's history a hundred years hence.'[13]

Of all the students that attended Brickendonbury, Rheam said that the Norwegians impressed him the most, for their readiness to run risks and for their steadiness in facing the dangers of sabotage. He was particularly impressed with the Gunnerside party. In his report he stated that

this was an excellent party in every way, and each member has a thorough knowledge of the target, and the methods of dealing with the different sections. Their demolitions work was exceedingly good and thorough and their weapon training outstanding. If the conditions are at all possible, they have every chance of carrying out the operation successfully.[14]

By this time, the SOE had realised that it was a better idea to equip the agents with white parachutes and white 'jump-suits' and not to send them in full military uniform. Round trips to the north of Norway were over 4,000 miles so refuelling was done at Kinloss or Lossiemouth in north-east Scotland. On 23 January 1943, Squadron Leader Gibson left Tempsford in a Halifax with the six Norwegian agents but failed to locate the DZ in the Telemark province of southern Norway. After an hour and a half searching they had to return to Kinloss. Another mission was planned. This time two teams were selected from the most experienced aircrew at Tempsford for Operation Gunnerside. The senior aircrew were doubled up – two pilots, two navigators, two rear gunners, etc. – the reason being that the return trip was so long that a single crew might have become overtired. Group Captain Ken Batchelor piloted one of the planes, Squadron Leader Gibson the other. Two Stirling IVs were allocated but only one was actually used; the other was in case the first became unserviceable at Kinloss. The planes took off on 16 February 1943. The actual drop was on a glacier that fed into Lake Skrykken in the north of Norway, near the Swedish border. John Charrot, a 138 Squadron pilot, recalled in his memoirs how Gibson's navigator did a great job using skilful dead reckoning navigation to hit exact landfall after 700 miles across the North Sea.

This successful landfall set the tone for the whole operation. It was now up to me and everyone else who could see the ground, to map read to the dropping zone. This was not an easy task. The tops of the mountains which are around 6,000 feet were covered in snow and ice and all the frozen lakes looked much like the last one we had flown over. We were after all trying to find a particular frozen lake on the Hardanger plateau. It was a really beautiful night. The moon was bright, the clouds were light and fluffy, and we could see a long way. At one time the rear gunner suggested that perhaps they were not pretty fluffy clouds, but the tops of mountains we were scudding over – he may well have been right. Because of the failure to find the lights and the dropping point on the previous trip, it had been decided that this time it would be a free drop on the Hardanger plateau. Then the party of six would ski with all their equipment to meet up with the four members of GROUSE. We were not convinced that the correct lake had been identified, but, as the drop was vital, the skipper and the Norwegian leader, Joachim Rønneberg, decided not to delay, so all the six brave young men and their packages were dropped. The rear gunner reported all parachutes had opened and we set off for the long haul to Tempsford. I can remember thinking, as we watched the parachutes going down onto this frozen waste land, what courage they had. We were returning to base for bacon and beans, but what was in store for them?[15]

Another crew member recalls the sheer beauty of the mountains that were completely snow-covered, the lakes in the moonlight and above all the Northern Lights when they flew close to the Arctic Circle. The whole trip was flown at a very low level, which required some very skilful flying. The area where the 'Joes' were dropped was so remote in the centre of the frozen Bjorn Fjord that they were fearful that there was no habitation and that perhaps the SOE people had got things wrong. They used Rebecca to assist in direction finding, got correct signals from the ground, three lights in the shape of the letter 'T' with the longer vertical line indicating which direction the wind was blowing and the horizontal the width of the DZ. Perhaps on the instructions of the passengers, they passed to the north of it and dropped them and five containers on the frozen surface of Bjorns Fjord 18 miles off target.

The six Norwegian agents parachuted into the worst blizzard any of them could remember with temperatures down to -20°C. Rønneberg, their leader, recalled the appalling weather conditions:

> Before the night was over it was a real blizzard and there was no question of leaving the hut at all, we just had to stay put until the weather improved. That took four days. I remember we had some ventilator on top of the chimney that was broken loose and I climbed up to try to fix it and I was twice lifted by the storm from the roof and thrown on the other side of the hut. That tells you a little bit about the strength of the wind.[16]

A week later, the weather improved enough for them to begin a 31-mile ski walk, hauling their supplies on a toboggan over difficult terrain to meet up with the reconnaissance team of Claus Helberg and Arne Kjelstrup. When supplies ran low they survived on reindeer meat and moss. Having wireless communication allowed them to eventually meet up and celebrate with chocolate, raisins and biscuits instead.

The attack on Vemork was planned for the night of 27 February. While at Brickendonbury, Tronstad had ensured that they knew the exact details of the terrain, the approaches and exits to the plant and exactly where to place the explosives and twenty-five-second fuses on the eighteen 4-foot-2-inch-high high-concentration cells and interconnecting pipework. They had constantly practised entering the building, placing and fixing the charges and making good their escape until the whole operation was reduced to just a few minutes. The only problem was access. Aerial photographs of the site showed the general layout of the buildings, the perimeter fence and the very difficult terrain. They also showed that the overhead power lines that entered the plant did so at about ground level, close to the heavy water plant. This information was vital as such cable entries were often unsealed and could provide access to the building.

The Norsk Hydro plant could only be reached on foot via a narrow, 75-foot-long suspension bridge spanning the gorge, along a single-track railway hewn into the side of the ravine and running directly into the plant, from above or down steep steps along pipes feeding water into the turbines from a reservoir at the top of the mountain. When Rønneberg sent one of the team down the 600-foot valley side to find somewhere to cross the River Maan, he returned with news that there was a crossable ice bridge. Hiding their skis for their getaway, they all undertook to use their L pill if they were wounded to allow the others to escape more quickly. The saboteurs chose a difficult rock climb down into the ravine below the dam under the cover of darkness. Laden with arms and stores, they crossed the half-frozen torrent and climbed up the other side to the unguarded railway line.

Once the guards changed, while Poulsson's team prepared to give covering fire and fight off any guards who appeared, Rønneberg's team cut their way through the perimeter fence using a pair of heavy bolt croppers, climbed through the cable entry and made their way inside the building with 11 pounds of explosives in their haversacks. Rønneberg detailed what happened next:

My colleague kept watch over the guard, who seemed frightened but was otherwise quiet and obedient. I began to place the charges. This went quickly and easily. The models on which we had practised in England were exact duplicates of the real plant. I had placed half the charges in position, when there was a crash of broken glass behind me. I looked up. Someone had smashed the window opening onto the backyard. A man's head stood framed in the broken glass. It was one of my colleagues. Having failed to find the cable tunnel, they had decided to act on their own initiative. One climbed through the window, helped me place the remaining charges and checked them twice while I coupled the fuse. We checked the entire charge once more, before ignition. There was still no sign of alarm from the yard.

When we were nearly finished putting up the charges we started talking about the fuses in Norwegian and the Norwegian guard suddenly said that he would be very pleased if he could have his glasses because they were so difficult to get in Norway those days. The natural answer would probably have been, damn your glasses. In the end I found the glasses case and said, 'Here you are', and he said, 'Thank you very much indeed.' I was down on the floor with insulating tape and so on, making up the last of the charges, ready for blowing and he said, 'Well, I am sorry but the glasses are not inside the case,' and I had another search and I found them as a bookmark in his logbook. It's amazing what you do in that sort of stress situation.[17]

The Germans had disregarded an attack from the torrent side so when the guards heard muffled explosions, they did not expect saboteurs. The party of nine agents managed to escape on their skis, having left a British 'Tommy' gun as a calling card. Five dispersed to play other roles in the resistance and the others escaped across the mountains into Sweden. Rønneberg's wireless message read, 'Attacked 0045 on 28.2.43. High concentration plant totally destroyed. All present. No fighting.'[18]

Major Rheam, when he was informed of the group's success, wrote to Colonel Wilson, the head of the Norwegian section, expressing the feelings of pride engendered by the action of the saboteurs. 'I think Gunnerside was a most magnificent show and I have suggested to Colonel Woolrych [the chief instructor at Beaulieu] that some "secure" version of the story should be told to all our students as an example for them to look up to.'[19]

About 1,000 pounds of heavy water were destroyed in the attack and production was halted for several months. Although embarrassing the German scientists for whom heavy water was as precious as gold, it was not as major a setback to their plans as Churchill and the SOE planners had hoped. Before the attack, the plant had been producing about 11 pounds of heavy water a day. When it was rebuilt, by June 1943 it was producing 14½ pounds a day. Although it stopped the Third Reich from building their atomic bomb before the Americans, it is claimed to have been a major influence in turning the attention of German scientists towards the development of their V rockets instead.

Another mission was planned when the SOE received wireless messages from their agents in Norway that production had restarted. When the Americans were told the news, they planned their own attack. On 16 November 1943, a bombing mission was undertaken involving 388 B-17 and B-24 bombers from the 8th Air Force. Over 700 500-pound bombs were dropped on the Vemork plant and 100 250-pound bombs on the town at Rjukan. Because of its position beneath the hydro-electric power station, only two of the bombs actually hit the electrolysis plant and the heavy water tanks were untouched. One bomb hit the civilian air-raid shelter in Vemork, killing eight men and fourteen women and children. The nitrate plant in nearby Rjukan was destroyed. When the Norwegian government-in-exile heard about the raid, they protested strongly because it had been carried out without their prior knowledge or approval.

Although only 120 pounds of heavy water were destroyed in the American attack, the German response was to abandon the Vemork plant and move the remaining components and stock and build heavy water separation plants in Bavaria and northern Italy. The remaining 3,600 gallons were planned to be transported in specially reinforced barrels to Mel, a ferry port on Lake Tinnsjø. They were to be loaded onto the ferry, the *Hydro*, and then shipped across the Skaggerak to Hamburg in Germany.

In a message Skinnarland sent to Tronstad, dated 9 February 1944, he informed him of the Germans' plans for transporting IMI, the code name for heavy water:

> AS MENTIONED BEFORE THE TIME IS SHORT AND CONSEQUENTLY IT IS DIFFICULT TO CARRY OUT AN ARMED ATTACK WHICH WOULD HAVE TO BE DIRECTED AGAINST THE STORE AT VEMORK BEFORE THEY HAVE GERMAN GUARDS. WE FIND THE SAFEST SOLUTION TO BE SINKING OF THE FERRY OF TINNSJOEN (TINN-LAKE) WITH ALL THE IMI BARRELS ABOARD THROUGH CIVILIAN SABOTAGE. MAY WE HAVE THE PERMISSION TO DO THIS? THE ONLY OTHER POSSIBILITY IS TO BLOW UP THE WHOLE TRAIN FOR EXAMPLE AT SVELGFOSS. WE MUST COUNT ON REPRISALS BOTH AFTER A MILITARY AND A CIVILIAN ACTION. REPLY SOONEST.[20]

Having discussed it with the Norwegian military authorities and SOE's Norwegian section, Tronstad replied the following day:

> AGREE TO SINKING OF FERRY IN DEEP WATER PREFERABLY BETWEEN HESLEVIKEN AND DIGERUD. IF THE SEA-COCKS ARE OPENED THIS MUST BE COMBINED WITH AN EXPLOSION TO INDICATE A LIMPET ATTACK FROM OUTSIDE. THE ENGINE MUST BE PUT OUT OF ORDER SO THAT THE FERRY CANNOT BE DRIVEN TO SHALLOW WATER. TWENTY NINE OF THE TENTH. THE SINKING MUST NOT FAIL AS THE METHOD OF ATTACK WILL THEREBY BE DISCLOSED. LEAVE BRITISH UNIFORM EFFECTS IF POSSIBLE AT SUITABLE PLACE. GOOD LUCK.[21]

Skinnarland discussed the operation with Haukelid, code-named BONZO, and on 16 February sent the following message:

BONZO SUBMITS THE FOLLOWING. REFERENCE IMI
LUT WHICH IS TO BE TRANSPORTED. A QUANTITY
CORRESPONDING TO ABOUT 400 KG OF FINISHED IMI
COULD BE DESTROYED OF WHICH THERE WILL BE 50
KG OF FINISHED IMI. OUR CONTACTS SAY THAT THE
GERMAN METHOD IS INFERIOR TO ELECTROLYSIS AND
THEY THEREFORE DOUBT WHETHER THE EFFECT OF
THE OPERATION IS WORTH THE REPRISALS WHICH MUST
BE RECKONED WITH. AS WE CAN NOT DECIDE HOW
IMPORTANT THE OPERATION IS WE REQUEST A REPLY
SOONEST IF POSSIBLE THIS EVENING. IMI SHIPS APPARENTLY
GO DIRECT TO HAMBURG. GREETINGS.[22]

Tronstad replied:

THE MATTER HAS BEEN CONSIDERED AND IT IS DECIDED THAT
IT IS VERY IMPORTANT TO DESTROY THE IMI. HOPE IT CAN BE
DONE WITHOUT TOO GREAT MISFORTUNE. WE SEND OUR BEST
WISHES FOR SUCCESS IN THE WORK. GREETINGS.[23]

When Haukelid discovered that the closely guarded railway trucks
carrying the consignment were to arrive at the little port on Sunday
afternoon, 20 February, he made plans. The Gunnerside team boarded
the *Hydro* at 0100 hours and Haukelid told the Norwegian guard that
he was on the run from the Gestapo. While one of them stood guard,
the other three wriggled through a hole in the floor and crept along the
keel up to the bows where they planted 19 pounds of high explosive in
the form of sausages in the cramped bilges in a foot of water. Two alarm
clock mechanisms with a third of an inch clearance in the loose contacts
were timed to go off at 10.45 a.m. when the ferry was over the deepest
part of the lake. They left the boat by 04.00 a.m. and were in Oslo that
afternoon. The *Hydro* duly sank, with the loss of fourteen Norwegians
and up to twenty Germans in 200 fathoms of water.

Witnesses reported seeing some barrels floating on the surface. An
examination of the records showed that some barrels were only half

full. When the incident was reported back to London, Tronstad was concerned in case the Germans had learned of the Gunnerside operation and had used dummy barrels. Although his contacts in Vemork said that barrels had been loaded, it was not until 2003 that an expedition by a team working on a science documentary for NOVA, a television company, confirmed that those on board contained the coveted compound.

The mission was considered so important to the Allies that, unknown to Haukelid, the SOE had a 'Plan B' in case the ferry was not sunk. This was a plan to attack the ferry at Herøya, a port facility near Porsgrunn on the south coast of Norway. Research by NOVA into Norsk Hydro's production records and analysis of an intact barrel that was retrieved from the lake indicates that the heavy water did not contain high concentrations of deuterium oxide. To have produced atomic weapons, German scientists would have needed to have enriched the heavy water. It was also argued that the quantity on board, about half a ton, was insufficient. It was claimed that 5 tonnes were needed to start a nuclear reactor and 10 tonnes to produce enough plutonium for a nuclear weapon.

The details of the Grouse, Freshman and Gunnerside operations remained secret until the end of the war. In 1948 a Norwegian/French film, *Kampen om tungtvannet/La Bataille de l'eau loured*, was released, which told the story, and in 1965 the film *The Heroes of Telemark*, starring Kirk Douglas and Richard Harris, provided a fictionalised account. Haugland described it as Hollywood nonsense with a lot of love and shooting. Ray Mears, the celebrity survival expert, helped produce a three-part BBC TV documentary 'The Real Heroes of Telemark' and wrote a book on the subject detailing the background, the operation itself and the aftermath.

Michael Foot, the SOE historian, made the point that this coup brought off in Norway changed the course of the war and was so important that nothing else the section did bore record beside it. It ended the Germans' overtaking the Allies in the race to produce the atomic bomb and has been described as the most successful sabotage operation of the Second World War, involving four attempts with the loss of ninety-two lives.

Rønneberg and Poulsson both received the Distinguished Service Order and the rest of the team either the Military Cross or, as the case of Stromsheim, the Military Medal. He was also awarded the French Legion of Honour and the Croix de Guerre. While the Norwegian members of Kompani Linge who undertook the sabotage became national heroes, one needs to acknowledge the role played by Brickendonbury in the liberation of Norway.

CHAPTER 7

Brickendonbury and Blackmail Sabotage: Peugeot Automobile Works, Sochaux-Montbéliard, France, 1943–4

In the first few years of the war, the SOE had difficulties persuading Lord Harris, the Marshal of the Royal Air Force, to divert aircraft engaged in the country's defence to the Special Duties Squadrons. Foot claimed that Harris was loath to supply them to carry ragamuffins to distant spots, in pursuit of objects no one seemed anxious to explain. Lord Portal, Chief of the Air Staff, told Harry Sporborg, the deputy head of SOE,

> Your work is a gamble which may give us a valuable dividend or may produce nothing ... My bombing offensive is not a gamble. Its dividend is certain; it is a gilt-edged investment. I cannot divert aircraft from a certainty to a gamble which may be a gold-mine or may be completely worthless.[1]

In November 1943, a new form of sabotage changed their minds. Termed the 'blackmail scheme', it involved industries being sabotaged with the complicity and assistance of their managements. They were offered immunity from aerial bombardment and subsequent loss of life on condition that 'the precise instructions issued by London for the destruction of key items of machinery, plant or stocks were carried out and that evidence that the required damage had been done was submitted immediately to London H.Q.'[2]

The first blackmail sabotage took place against the Peugeot works in Sochaux-Montbéliard in the Strasbourg region of eastern France. There had been little sabotage undertaken in this area largely due to the enemy's concerted efforts to Germanise the population. Pierre de Vomecourt had been parachuted into the area in May 1941 to assist his brother, Baron Jean de Vomecourt, who had built up many contacts in the Société Nationale des Chemins de Fer Français (SNCF). They organised teams of railwaymen to be ready for the Allies' instructions to cut all communications between France and Germany when the expected Second Front, the Allied invasion, started. However, in early 1942, Pierre was arrested along with other members of his network and transported to a German concentration camp.

One of those arrested was Captain Hudson, who was in charge of the area around Clermont-Ferrand. His second-in-command, Captain Rafferty, code-named Aubretia, took over this group but it was not until 14/15 April 1943 that the SOE sent in another organiser. This was twenty-nine-year-old Harry Rée, a French and German teacher who had lived and worked in north-east France before the war. In 1940 he registered as a conscientious objector and worked for the National Fire Service. However in 1941, having learned about the Nazis' treatment of the Jews, he re-registered for military service and was called up to join the Army. His language skills drew him to the attention of the SOE, who appointed him a captain in the Intelligence Corps. Acting as a conducting officer to Soviet NKVD agents, he quickly learned about the work of SOE. Realising he could speak better French than some of the agents about to be sent into the field, he volunteered for active service. On 14 September, he attended the assessment course at Wanborough Manor (STS 5), near Guildford in Surrey, and his instructor commented that he was

dissatisfied with this work, as not offering sufficient scope for his energies and desire to get on with the job. Speaks good French and German at 'School standard' fluently but incorrectly. Physical and moral courage to an unusually high degree. Sportsman and athlete; leader; popular at all times; very tolerant of other people but apt to lose his 'sense of military hierarchy' in face of incompetence or neglect of duty, on the part of his superiors. Needs a good deal of hard work and liberty to keep him happy. Puts everything into subjects and schemes in which he is interested; Falls asleep frankly and unashamedly when not. Very good influence on other trainees.[3]

After his paramilitary training at Meoble Lodge (STS 23) in Inverness-shire he was reported as 'strong as the hills'. The comment on his explosives and demolitions training was that he had 'good sound knowledge. Not particularly outstanding but good enough to instruct fairly advanced demolitions. He had a poor memory and forgets quickly. Interested in the work and has tried hard to get his knowledge up to instructing standard.' His French was reported to have improved and, despite leaving papers and money around, which raised issues about his sense of security, he was considered a reliable student.[4] After attending the Finishing School at The Rings (STS 31) at Beaulieu, Lieutenant-Colonel Woolrych, the Station Commandant, reported that he was,

very intelligent and intellectual, very quick but not very practical. In spite of the fact that he is hard working and enthusiastic, his excellent mental qualities are seriously marred by a natural erraticism which leads him to gross carelessness. He has a strong character and a deep sense of honour and duty, but, at the same time, he is highly strung and nervy. He is an uncompromising idealist and would be quite ruthless with anyone who roused his moral disapproval. He is very tactless and hates authority as such. Nevertheless, he would always be a loyal subordinate for idealistic rather than disciplinary reasons. He has an exasperating personality which many people might find intolerable, but, nevertheless, those who understand him like him very much. In spite of these feelings he has certain powers of leadership and would win him the respect of those who understand him. Although he would probably be the last to admit it, he is very apprehensive about the work he has volunteered to undertake. He has serious doubts as to whether he is mentally capable of carrying it out. He is worried about his French. As a result of this he has of late slept badly and those who have known him previously were shocked by his change of appearance. All instructors here agree that he is not suited, either mentally or temperamentally for the work for which he is intended, and feel very strongly that he should not be so employed. He is not good at Codes and Ciphers and requires further practice. On account of his innate carelessness it is doubtful whether he will ever be really good at this work.[5]

Although there was no instructor's report for him having attended the Basic Course at Brickendonbury, in an interview outside the house for a 1984 BBC documentary on the SOE he mentioned that while he was there he was taken to Hitchin station to look at ways of destroying steam trains. He showed where to place the explosive on the front of the cylinder and commented that French trains were easier to blow up than British ones.[6]

Even though his wife was expecting their second child, he agreed to be parachuted into France with the SOE agreeing to send him the sentence 'Clément ressemble au grand-père' or 'Clémence ressemble à la grand-mère' in the *messages personnels* broadcast after the news on the BBC's French service to let him know. Given documents in the name of Henri Rayon, code-named Cesar, he was allocated Amédée Maingard, code-named Dédé, as his wireless operator. His was a sabotage mission with targets of Bergougnan and Michelin at Clermont-Ferrand; Dunlop at Montlucon; transformers surrounding Clermont-Ferrand and railways between Limoges and Brives, Vierson and Montlucon, Moulins and Bridode and Besançon and Bourg.

On the night of 14 April 1943, they were taken in one of the Special Duties Squadron's modified Whitley bombers and parachuted into the Sarrouilles Hills, about 4 miles east of Tarbes, near Lourdes. The despatcher, according to Maingard, did not give the instructions to jump loud enough so they landed off target with no reception committee to meet them. One of their containers had got caught in overhead transmission lines. Unable to carry all the supplies, Maingard took his wireless set and Rée rescued one of the suitcases, which he hoped would contain chocolates and cigarettes for the Resistance. Wearing heavy greatcoats over their French clothes, they made their way through the woods, following a stream to throw the dogs that were barking off their scent.

In the morning, Maingard went off to rendezvous with the reception committee working in Maurice Southgate's Stationer network. The Hotel Normandie, where he was supposed to meet his contact, had been requisitioned as the Gestapo HQ so he had to try the second address he had been given. While he was away, Rée was found by one of the locals. Pretending he was an escaped English soldier, he convinced the man to help him, and he brought ham, cheese, bread and wine, which helped sustain him until Maingard returned the following day with a bicycle. The suitcase he had taken only contained tins of lubricating oil for machine guns.

Rée's mission was to help Rafferty develop the contacts he had made in Dijon and in the Doubs and Jura regions. Using a safe house in Tarbes, Rée was contacted by Jacqueline Nearne, Maurice Southgate's courier, who had been sent to escort him to Clermont-Ferrand. On 5 May, while staying in a safe house, he heard the message 'Clémence ressemble à la grand-mère'.

When Jacqueline introduced him to Michel, the local Resistance leader, he was reported not to have been impressed with Rée's French. He thought it had an obvious English accent, which would be dangerous in a city with so many Gestapo and collaborators. Instead, he was sent to the Belfort-Dijon area where he organised parachute drops. On 17 May, he learned that Rafferty had been arrested. Just over a fortnight later George Jones, another SOE agent, was captured. As there was an informer in the area, on 25 July Rée used the services of a *passeur* to guide him across the border into Switzerland where he contacted the British Embassy in Berne. On sending his report, he and others in his network were ordered to lie low until the man concerned was 'liquidated'.

When he first arrived in France, his cover story was that he was training to be a priest in Paris, which he felt did not explain the numerous journeys he would have to make. His contacts acquired new papers identifying him as a farm labourer but he did not think this role would explain him travelling by bicycle to different towns and villages. Instead, he was provided with documents identifying him as André Blied, one of a well-known watchmaking family in Besançon. Another of his concerns was the clothes he had been provided with. His socks wore out after two days and the soles of the shoes he was issued with had been made with some paper substance which wore out rapidly. He later suggested to HQ that saboteurs ought to be provided with dungarees as they would allow them to enter factories without exciting suspicion.[7]

He was sent to the Lons-le-Saunier area with John Young, a wireless operator, and 'Chaplain', a courier, to join a group of Maquis living in the foothills of the Jura Mountains in eastern France. Following the introduction of the *Service du Travail Obligitaire* in March 1943, the Nazis expected half a million French workers would be sent to work in German industries. Those unwilling to comply with the order either tried to leave the country or move into the hills. The SOE recognised that these groups of Maquis could make a valuable contribution to the Allies' plans if they were armed and trained. Rée helped locate suitable drop zones and arranged for the Special Duties Squadrons to parachute food, clothing, money, weapons, ammunition, explosives and other supplies. He also provided the men with instruction in arms and sabotage and helped set up the Acrobat network.

On being informed that there were groups in nearby towns and villages who were keen to receive arms and supplies, engage in train derailments and blow up canal lock gates, he felt he could help them. The SOE agreed as the canals in the area were being used to transport small U-boats from Germany down to the Mediterranean.

When he arrived in Montbéliard, he was introduced to André van der Straten, an ex-French Army lieutenant who was a foreman in the Peugeot works in Sochaux and ran a small resistance group. Using Maingard's wireless set, Rée sent encoded messages back to London organising supply drops to a field near Valentigney, a few kilometres south of Sochaux.

Following the arrest of Dominique, the head of his Maquis group, SOE decided that Rée and André should form a new network named Stockbroker. Acrobat was taken over with the arrival on 17 May of Captain John Starr and John Young, another wireless operator.[8] Aware of increased German activity in the area, Rée and André had to get away. Pushing their bicycles through a wood and lifting them when the undergrowth became too dense, four hours later they arrived at the village of Montbéliard where they hid. Safe for the moment, they started plotting an attack on Peugeot's huge automobile works in nearby Sochaux, which was run by André's friend, Rodolphe Peugeot. Employing about 60,000 workers, the factory had been taken over by the Germans and retooled to manufacture military vehicles, tank turrets, tank engines and tank tracks for the Wehrmacht and components for aircraft engines for the Luftwaffe. As a result, it was number three on the RAF's list of important industrial targets in France.

In the meantime, once they had trained some men, on 3 June he completed the first part of his mission. Accompanied by two men, he entered the Michelin tyre plant in Clermont-Ferrand, overpowered the two French guards and threw six incendiaries into a barn containing 5,000 truck tyres. In his debrief he claimed that 'there was an enormous conflagration in which all the tyres were completely destroyed', thus denying them for use on the German's military vehicles.[9] Foot reported over 300 tons of rubber being destroyed.[10]

To assist Rée, Diane Rowden was dropped on 17 June to act as his courier, carrying messages to various people in his network and bringing their replies back. In another attack, one of his teams blew up six locomotive cylinders between Dijon and Dôle and, on 15 July, they derailed a train at Vonjeaucourt and destroyed a dump of 6,030 lorry tyres.

That night, on the train from Besançon to Montbéliard, Rée witnessed the RAF's first raid on the Peugeot works at Sochaux. 165 Halifax bombers were involved in the attack. When the first bombs fell, locals fled into the fields and the Germans fired red flares, which some pilots mistook for markers. As a result 700 bombs fell on residential and business areas in what Rée called 'Peugeot city', Sochaux, Old

Carmont, Nommay and Etupes Allenjoie, as well as in nearby fields where people were hiding. 125 were killed and 250 injured. 100 houses were completely destroyed, 200 were uninhabitable and 200 partially damaged. The *mairie* (town hall), the school, post office and the police barracks were totally destroyed. The main roads were blocked and the Rhone-Rhine canal burst. A RAF report admitted that five planes were shot down and only 5 per cent of the factory was damaged. Only thirty bombs hit the factory. The forging and stamping suffered very little; the foundry and body shop were seriously affected and the mechanical workshop was destroyed. The attack was considered a failure as production continued as normal.[11]

Faced with such a disaster, the Peugeot family bought stocks of food to feed the homeless. They provided 10 tons of potatoes, 3 tons of carrots, 5 tons of cabbage, 900 kg of mixed vegetables, 200 kg of fat, 180 kg of rice, 240 kg of flour, 700 kg of dough, about 2 and a half tons of bread, 700 kg of jam, 300 kg of chocolate and about 5,000 litres of wine.[12] Rée reported that there was no anti-British feeling:

> The French were anticipating a second front, the allied invasion ...
> It is a horrid thing to say but what impresses them most is the death
> of allied personnel, whether it be bomb victims or aviators, and
> consequently they appreciate those who risk death, like them. This
> sympathy with the allies assumes gigantic proportions when they can
> see with their own eyes living proof of this common suffering and
> common risk taking. Hence the bounteous help to escaping airmen
> and the almost embarrassing and fantastic funeral arrangements for
> the unlucky ones.[13]

Rée learned that while these attacks were turning some French citizens against the British and decreasing their support for the Resistance, there were others who were more sympathetic to the Allied cause. He came up with an alternative plan. In Major R. A. Bourne-Paterson's *British Circuits in France 1941–1944*, he stated that

In early July 1943, Henri [Rée] made his first contact with the Peugeot management in the person of Paul Sire, Director of Coordination of all Peugeot factories, who proved a valuable contact. He told him that the management were already toying with the idea of sabotaging their own factory in order to stop production and prevent another disastrous RAF bombing attack. From Henri's point of view, this was just what he wanted to hear.[14]

Managing to get through numerous secretarial intermediaries, he was able to speak on the telephone to Rodolphe Peugeot, a young, amiable director of the works, and made an appointment to see him that night. Maurice Buckmaster, the head of SOE's F Section, in his fictionalised accounts of agents he sent into France, commented in his story about Rée that

> The Peugeots lived in considerable luxury, for the factory was doing well in the service of the Boches. It cannot be concealed that a large number of French industrialists were finding it very rewarding to co-operate with the Germans; in Robert Peugeot's case, however, it was with the greatest reluctance. For a long time he had resisted strong pressure to turn his factory over to war production and had only given in when threatened with expropriation and the removal to Germany of his trained technicians.[15]

When Rée explained that he and some of his friends wanted to blow up his factory, Peugeot was shocked. Telling him that he was a British officer was met with disbelief; Peugeot was worried that he might be a German provocateur trying to get him to say something incriminating. To prove his credentials, Rée asked Peugeot if he listened to the BBC and, on learning that he did only occasionally, in two days' time he offered to get any phrase he could think of included among the BBC French service's *messages personnels,* which were broadcast after the evening news. 'La guerre de Troie n'aura pas lieu' (The Trojan War will not take place) was suggested and Rée arranged for it to be included in Maingard's 'sked', his scheduled transmission, that night.

When Rée heard the message a few days later, he called at Peugeot's home to find out if he had. Ushered into an expensively furnished sitting room hung with tapestries, he overheard German voices coming from the next room. Opening the window, he saw an interior courtyard but, before he climbed out, he overheard Peugeot saying farewell to them by the front door. When he came in and saw Rée by the open window, he asked if he was about to make a run for it. The Germans, he explained, were a trade delegation who wanted to look over the factory and he had suggested that they listened to the ridiculous things played on the BBC. He told Rée that they laughed like pigs at the silly messages. Buckmaster continued their conversation.

> 'I will tell you quite frankly what the position is. The people in London want the Peugeot factory put out of action. They will bomb you, they say, unless production can be stopped within a short time. Now if they bomb you there will be much loss of life among your workers. They live very close to the factory, a lot of them, and there would certainly be heavy casualties. Now if you were to let a few of my men get into the factory one dark night …'
>
> 'I am to destroy my own factory? My dear man …'
>
> 'One way or another it will be destroyed. If we do it there will be few casualties and furthermore we can put the explosive where it will do the greatest harm to production and the least to the fabric of the factory. If the R.A.F. bomb you the whole place will be smashed to smithereens. The cause of the Allies will be better served if you let us do it and in the long run you will suffer less.'[16]

Peugeot found Rée's argument to be very persuasive. Despite being sympathetic to the Resistance, he had had no alternative but to comply with the Germans' demands or face the expropriation of his machinery and the transfer of his technicians to Germany. It also guaranteed the livelihoods of his workers.

Not mentioned by Buckmaster was Rée asking Peugeot for a loan of 100,000 francs, which he promised the SOE would reimburse by placing the amount into a bank account in his name in London.

1. Brickendonbury Manor in the early 1950s. (Courtesy of the Tun Abdul Razak Research Centre)

2. Kim Philby, the SIS officer who created the first curriculum for the 'D School' at Brickendonbury. (Courtesy of cyberboris.wordpress.com)

3. Frederick 'Fritz' Peters, VC, DSO, DSC and Bar, DSC American, RN, Brickendonbury's first commandant. (Courtesy of Sam McBride)

4. Cecil 'Nobby' Clarke, MC, replaced Captain Peters as Brickendonbury's commanding officer in 1940. He developed a range of explosive devices like limpets, spigot bombs and altimeter switches. (Courtesy of Mrs John Clarke)

5. One of Brickendonbury's students demonstrating how Nobby Clarke's early limpet bombs could be carried. (Courtesy of Mrs John Clarke)

6. Examining a ball-bearing sabotage. (TNA HS 7/135)

7. Saboteur placing explosives on a railway line. (TNA HS 7/135)

8. The location of the Norsk Hydro heavy water plant at Rjukan, Norway. (Courtesy of Hydro Vemork, Rjukan)

9. Another view of the Norsk Hydro heavy water plant at Rjukan, Norway. (Courtesy of Hydro Vemork, Rjukan)

10. Another view of the location of the Norsk Hydro heavy water plant at Rjukan, Norway. (Courtesy of Hydro Vemork, Rjukan)

11. Several of the high-concentration cells destroyed in the attack on the Norsk Hydro heavy water plant on 27/28 February 1943. (Courtesy of Hydro Vemork, Rjukan)

SURVEILLANCE des USINES par les Waffen S.S.

A la suite des attentats commis dans les usines de Sochaux, les autorités allemandes ont décidé de faire exercer une surveillance supplémentaire des usines et du personnel employé.

Cette surveillance est exercée par les Waffen S.S. armés (uniforme : béret basque, canadienne kaki, pantalon bleu) qui ont reçu, de la part de leur commandement, des instructions très fermes.

En particulier, toute personne interpellée doit présenter quel que soit l'endroit où elle se trouve la carte d'identité PEUGEOT ainsi que dans certains endroits particuliers des laissez-passer spéciaux.

Les Waffen S.S. peuvent contrôler le contenu des paquets et des poches.

A toute demande des Waffen S.S. les paquets devront être ouverts et les poches de vêtements vidées et retournées.

SOCHAUX, le 22 Mars 1944.

AFFICHAGE JUSQU'AU 15 AVRIL 1944.

12. A Waffen SS poster from the Peugeot works at Sochaux.

146.

APPENDIX II(f).

Form T.H.S.4.

FINISHING REPORT.
(To be submitted in duplicate to S.T.S. H.Q.)

S.T.S. No....17......   Party..........

Name by which known..............   School No......

Grade..............

Particulars of Finishing Training given:

Standard basic course in Industrial Sabotage including Steam and Hydro-Electric Power Stations, Transmission Systems, Engineering Factories, Steam and Electric Railways and Road Transport. Some instruction was also given in the Iron and Steel Industries.

Instruction was also given in Military Targets and in the prevention of Demolitions. Demolitions and P.T. were also included.

Report:

GENERAL.   A hardworking student who made very good progress with the technical subjects. He seems to have gained a sound grasp of our methods.

MECHANICAL SUBJECTS.   Showed great interest in these subjects and with a little more practice should become very good at recognition and attack. He understands our methods well.

ELECTRICAL SUBJECTS.   Made good progress and has a sound knowledge of electrical equipment. He understands the methods of attack.

TRANSPORT   Worked well during lectures and should have a good understanding of the subject.

DEMOLITIONS.   Good.

P.T.   Fair.

SCHEMES.   Showed himself to be quite a capable leader although he needs more practice in preparing orders. He has the right spirit and should do well.

Date..................   Signed...................
                            Commandant.

13. Exemplar of an instructor's report for students at Brickendonbury. (TNA HS 8/371)

SECRET

BSS/I/400.

10th July, 1944.

Source is a Frenchman who, from 1929 to 1943 worked in the Peugeot Factories. He was recruited by a sabotage circuit and helped to organise, and occasionally carry out, sabotage of certain machinery at the Peugeot Works. He left France in April, 1944.

Interrogator's impression of source.

A Frenchman of average intelligence who is obviously very keen on his work. He is not given to exaggeration of his achievements, and seemed careful and truthful in his statements.

THE PEUGEOT FACTORIES AT SOCHAUX (DOUBS).

1. DESTRUCTION OF MACHINERY.

Source was asked about the destruction of certain machinery, and, in giving the following information, he stressed the fact that he was technical assistant in the coach-building section of the factory, and knew very little about technical expressions used in connection with engineering. He also knew little about the operations in which he had not taken part, although in most cases he had supplied the material. It was the custom for workmen to come to him for material with which to destroy certain machines, but often he never saw the men again or heard the results of the operation.

Machine	Method of Attack	Result.
Turbo-Compressors and Electric motors. a) 600 H.P.	Carried out by a team detailed by source. A magnetic mine placed on top of the compressor.	Each machine out of action for 6 months.
b) 2500 H.P.	One kilo of plastic placed in an opening at the base of the compressor.	
Gas Producer Plant.	Carried out by source who entered the factory dressed as a workman. A large magnetic under-water mine with 4 hrs. delay placed at the base under the water.	Out of action for 6 weeks.
Inside Transformer.	500 grammes of plastic pushed in a corner of the fins (ailettes)	Unknown.
Sand Dryers.	Carried out by some friends of source. 800 grammes of 808 placed in the ovens with cordtex detonators and time pencils.	Out of action for 1½ months.
Electricity Switchboard.	Carried out by a team. No further details known.	Out of action for 3 weeks.
Accumulators.	Material provided by source.	No information.
Milling machine for tank track tooth.	Magnetic mine provided by source.	No information.

14. Details of the sabotage on the Peugeot automobile works in Sochaux-Montbéliard, France, 1943–4. (TNA HS 9/1240/3)

Machine	Method of attack.	Result.
Boring Machine	Plastic provided by source. The workmen who carried out this operation understood the machine and put the explosive where they knew it would do most damage.	Out of action for 3 months. As it was a German one it could not be replaced.
High precision "Churchill" Grinding Machine	Magnetic mine provided by source.	No information.
Special lathe for F.W. Wing parts.	Magnetic mine provided by source.	No information.
Turret lathes.	Magnetic mine placed in the inside of the gears.	Out of use for 3 weeks, and as they were German, had to be sent back to Germany for repair. Efforts made to substitute various types of borrowed machines unsuccessful

2. OTHER SABOTAGE.

(i) In March 1944, magnetic mines were placed in the gears of two rectifying machines which had been brought from Germany and were in the process of being set up.

(ii) In February 1944, some of source's friends destroyed some lathes which had just arrived from Germany, and were standing in the yard of the factory.

(iii) Source himself was responsible for the destruction of 6000 tyres, and in March 1944 he blew up the high tension cables.

(iv) Sabotage was carried out of various replacements and parts sent from Germany. Source told the story of a consignment of springs for tanks which left Germany sealed up, and arrived at the factory with the seals broken and most of the contents missing. Source knew no more about the incident or about any similar acts of sabotage.

3. SABOTAGE TEAMS.

The sabotage was carried out by specially qualified workmen recruited by source and his organiser. Two engineers were in command, and they detailed workmen to do each particular job. There was also a team of mechanics who kept a look-out for suitable machines to be attacked. When machines arrived, the team leader took the necessary material from the stock of plastic mines, etc., which were stored in the factory, and when the work had been done, sent a report of the damage to source's organiser.

In January, 1944, source had conveyed 40 kilos of material - plastics, mines, etc. into the factory.

4. TRANSFORMERS.

Up to the time of source's departure, the main transformers had not been attacked. They were very heavily guarded by 20 Germans, and although the possibility of attacking them had been considered, it was decided that the loss of life among the attackers would be too great. They would have to force an entry and fight with men armed with machine guns, whereas they had only mitraillettes. Source had asked for mortars to be sent, as it was only with such a weapon that these transformers could be attacked, but he left just when they arrived.

15. Details of the sabotage on the Peugeot automobile works in Sochaux-Montbéliard, France, 1943–4. (TNA HS 9/1240/3)

To prove his credentials, Rée asked Peugeot for another phrase that he would get played in the *messages personnels*. Maingard sent the message 'La vallée du Doubs est belle, en été' (The Doubs valley is beautiful in the summer'), which was broadcast as promised. Peugeot handed over the money and after that they became quite good friends.[17]

Peugeot gave Rée a job as a technical assistant in the coach-building section of the Sochaux works and put him in touch with Roger Fouillette, an ex-Artillery Captain and local schoolteacher who was involved with the local resistance. Through him he was introduced to Pierre Lucas, the chief electrician at the works, who was wildly enthusiastic when Rée detailed how sabotaging only vital machinery could put the works out of action without anyone being injured. Delighted with this possibility, Lucas provided Rée with overalls and under the watchful eyes of the German guards, showed him all over the factory.[18] In Rée's debrief he stated that

> his training at STS 17 at this juncture proved invaluable to him, as it enabled him adequately to understand various technical considerations which had to be taken into account in order to carry out the sabotage. Source said that it would have been of little value to blow up the main transformer at Sochaux for the following reason:- High tension current was passed first through the transformer d'Etupes and then the reduced current was carried through the main transformer to small transformers which were situated in and supplied two shops in the factory. There was, however, also a direct line from the transformer d'Etupes to the small transformers situated in each of the remaining shops and they were supplied through this line direct from the transformer d'Etupes to the two shops that were fed by the main transformer. It was therefore essential in order materially to interfere with the work of the factory to destroy the transformer d'Etupes. Source stated that the transformer d'Etupes was guarded so heavily that it would have been impracticable to carry out sabotage against it because it was surrounded by barbed wire fences and there was a guard of some 20 Germans always on

duty. It would only be possible to attack this transformer from the air.[19]

In Buckmaster's account he mentioned that Rée and two of his friends in the Resistance were taken to the part of the factory where

> Harry knew by his training in England that the explosive would do the greatest damage. Certain machines were virtually irreplaceable under about six months it was upon these that the dynamiters would concentrate. Peugeot himself knew nothing further of the operation, but he gave them every co-operation, though he was kept out of the inner workings of the plan. Obviously security could not be relaxed in his favour and he had to be treated like any other outsider. He knew neither how nor when his factory would be knocked out, only that it would be.
>
> Harry and two of his gang were signed on as hands and thus were able to get in and out of the factory without exciting comment. They became thoroughly conversant with the machinery which they were to sabotage and, on the pretence of explaining its workings, the foremen were able to learn from Harry the vulnerable spots where explosive would do the most damage; Harry remembered with the utmost clarity the many hours he had spent in a Hertfordshire 'school' studying the weak spots of presses and lathes.[20]

Informing London of what he planned, the SOE gained the grudging, if conditional, agreement of the Air Ministry to postpone any further attacks on what was rapidly becoming their favourite target. The RAF's condition was that really effective sabotage had to be done on the ground.

Before the sabotage plans were made, Pierre Sire showed Rée a sketch of a 'flying bomb', the VI rocket, which Jean Pierre Peugeot had been given by one of his engineers who had stolen it during a business trip to Fallersleben. Rée arranged to meet the engineer for more information and, immediately afterwards, went to Switzerland to pass on the information to the British delegation. Peugeot had given him details of a *passeur* who guided him across the border. He acknowledged how invaluable the paramilitary training he had received in the Scottish mountains had been but commented in his report that there could be practical lessons on crossing borders.

When he returned, he began more sabotage training but the start of the operation was dependent on supplies being dropped. Rée admitted that the first acts of sabotage were partly in revenge for the Gestapo arresting 160 people in the Belfort-Montbéliard area on 26 October. 'The arrests acted like a coup de masse on the morale of the region. We decided, those of us who were left, that it was essential to make bangs and fires everywhere as soon as possible. We were very short of means of initiation.'[21]

Rée's request to the SOE that they arranged a pseudo raid by two Mosquito planes to disguise their sabotage was not permitted. However, they sent him the following message:

We are delighted at suggestion of Management which we accept. R.A.F. willing to defer attack until your attempt, assuming this will be made more or less immediately. R.A.F. had intended operations this moon but in any case, will not now go until November. In order to convince R.A.F. how much better this system is, can you send photos or other evidence of damage which will not be released to press or public? Similar suggestions might then be made to other managements by our officers in order to couple maximum effective damage with minimum of loss French lives. Assuming wholesale co-operation of Management, insist following vulnerable points must be destroyed:
a) Mechanical drop hammers
b) Acetylene generating plant – method: fire
c) Special welding machines, if any
d) Large transformers
e) Air compressors – method: H.E. charges in H.P. cylinders and shaft bearings. Large compressor is driven by special motor taking current at 9000 volts five pounds each here on bearings and between armature and field winding.

f) Gas producers – method: ten pounds H.E. in generators. If large
quantities explosives available, go for gantries gears and grinding
machines. Management can suggest other spots where damage can be
done by explosion, fire.[22]

The first attempt did not go according to plan. On 31 October, he and
a group of men entered a depot containing 100 new Buicks about to be
converted into Wehrmacht cars. They laid a trail of phosphorous slabs
they had stolen from the Germans and linked up all the cars to a pile
of cushions by the door in which were two large incendiary bombs.
They only had one box of twelve-hour time pencils left, which had been
pressed nine hours earlier. On inspection, they found that most had
already gone off. They attached the others, taking out the safety pins
and retreating to safety, only to discover that they did not detonate the
charge.

Another of his teams planted incendiary bombs in the sawmill at
Maiche, about 20 miles south of Montbéliard, which put it out of action
for a month. They also derailed a train at Luzy and at the beginning
of November they destroyed two locomotives and two trains in Dôle
station.[23] An attack on a barge carrying cement was less successful. The
four-hour delay on the limpet took six hours to go off, holed the barge
but did not sink it. Although a bargee was killed, most of the cement
was saved.[24]

At 17.30 on 3 November 1943, the first attack on the Peugeot works
was launched. The leader of the group had been forced to go into
hiding following arrests the previous week so Rée had to coach André
as a replacement. Supplied with explosives and time pencils, André
led a party of six workmen into the factory. Wearing fake moustaches
and guards' armbands, they carefully placed twenty-one charges on
the transformers with a thirty-minute delay but those sent to blow
up the compressors had left the detonators behind. They hurriedly
left the works but were seen by a guard who raised the alarm. They
waited for the explosions but nothing happened. André's subsequent
examination revealed that the Germans had inspected the transformers
and removed the charges. He admitted that, even after Rée's detailed

instructions, the time pencils had been inserted the wrong way round. Rée blamed himself for not repeating the instructions to ensure he'd fully understood.[25]

Learning from their mistakes meant the next attempt had a greater chance of success. An attack was planned to destroy the company's gazogène trucks, vehicles powered by burning charcoal as almost all French coal was exported to Germany. However, he only had six half-hour pencils, which were needed for another job. On 4 November, one of his teams attacked the transformers at Fonderies Le Roy. In his report he stated,

> Two 350 kw transfos in brick building 5 metres by 5 metres. One kilo charge on one transfo only. Delay: one metre Bickford. Result: One transfo completely destroyed. Second can be repaired in 3 months (sent to Alsthom). Brick building laid flat and pulverised. Steel door thrown 25 metres. (These renseignements from official of Ponts et Chausees on spot).[26]

Whether it was Rée's intention to commemorate the execution of Guy Fawkes is unknown, but on 5 November 1943 the second attack on the Peugeot factory was launched (Buckmaster erroneously dated it as 14 May). In an interview after the war, Rée admitted that

> they decided they'd blow up a whole transformer house where all the electricity came into the factory. About five men were involved, Frenchmen who worked in the factory. They had their pistols in the pockets of their overalls and they had their explosives, plastic blocks with room for a detonator, in their pockets too. There was a wonderful carelessness about the whole thing. They were playing football with the German guards outside the transformer house – somebody had forgotten to get the key – and in playing football one of them dropped his plastic block of explosive and one of the German guards who was playing football pointed it out to him. 'You've dropped something, sir, I think.' He put it back in his pocket. That was absolutely typical.[27]

What was not mentioned was their disguises – fake moustaches, glasses and cotton stuffed into their cheeks.[28] Buckmaster provided further details in his account:

> Three operatives remained in the factory after the other workers had left. Soon after knocking-off time, two foremen let themselves in with their pass-keys and returned to the shop-floor which they had only just left. They liberated the three men who were shut in a cleaner's cupboard on the executive floor and took from it several large boxes labelled 'cleaning materials'. The contents of these boxes were tubular containers of scouring powder. The tops of these containers were unscrewed and several long sticks of explosive were revealed. Some flat tins contained plastic explosive which could be fastened to machinery rather like sticking plaster. The five men made their way downstairs to the night-watchman's room. This was no longer used. The Germans set their own guard on the place. The men could hear them forming up outside.
>
> The five ate their sandwiches and settled themselves to wait for the darkness. At eleven o'clock they moved to their prearranged stations in various sections of the factory. Harry and one of the foremen set their explosives in place, working with quiet detachment. The other men, under the other foreman, were engaged similarly in another sector of the shop floor. By midnight the agreed time all the explosive was in place. The ten-minute fuses were set and the five men hurried down to a disused side door of which one of the foremen knew. They came out into a deserted yard at the back of the factory. Another door was unlocked by the foreman's pass-key and they were out of the factory in a side alley. They all shook hands and hurried away: they had to get home as quickly as they could, for curfew had started and there would be a terrific turn-out of police and military as soon as the factory went up.
>
> At about ten minutes past midnight the shop-floor of the Peugeot factory was rent by several violent explosions. Fires were started and equipment so ruined that production was suspended indefinitely. There was nothing the Germans could do to incriminate Robert Peugeot

or any of the staff of whom five were missing. The two foremen had decided to join the Rée group rather than risk arrest by resuming their work. It was upon Harry and the others that the full fury of the authorities was directed. An intensive search was begun.[29]

In Rée's report on the incident to SOE, he stated,

> 1800 hrs. Compressors and motors stank. Turbo huge hole in side. Leaves twisted to blazes. Coussinet pulverised. 8,000 hp motor irreparable. One auxiliary compressor holed, and motor smashed. Charge on other auxiliary did not function. Motor smashed. 2245 first gazogène charge goes off. 2315 second gazogène charge goes off. Delays (4 hrs) had been screwed down at 1700 hrs. For results see photos, and I wish you could see faces of German Guards, and compare them with faces of workers, directors and population of Sochaux.[30]

He suggested that precision sabotage would be a much more efficient and less risky way of putting the works out of operation. According to Foot, the factory was out of production for three months.[31]

Using Rée's reports, photographs (which were not included in his file) and Peugeot's production figures, and carefully studying aerial photographs taken by RAF reconnaissance planes, Buckmaster succeeded in convincing 'Bomber' Harris at Bomber Command HQ that the SOE was capable of blowing up targets that Harris had maintained were better left to his air crews.[32]

An anonymous note in Rée's file stated that

> His action has opened up a new possibility for attaining the desired results of denial to the enemy of important factories without the intervention of the RAF. These results could not have been achieved without the personal intervention of Captain REE and his unfailing courage in the face of the most difficult and dangerous circumstances has been an inspiration to all who have been in contact with him.[33]

The Germans' response to the attack was to put sabotage guards in place and arrest a number of Resistance-supporting directors, managers and workers. After interrogation they were deported to Germany. Among them was Roger Fouillette. When Rée called on Madame Fouillette, she was nervous about his presence. One imagines he gave her money as it was the SOE's policy to financially help the families of Resistance members who had been arrested. She told him that the Gestapo had brought her husband back to the house and asked her if she knew the whereabouts of an Englishman. When they threatened to shoot her husband in front of her, she admitted knowing Henri but told them that he had fled to Switzerland and intended to remain there. In fact, he recommended she be awarded an MBE for the assistance she had provided him.

Conscious that the Germans would be aware of his activities, Rée decided to cross the border into Switzerland and await further instructions from London. Correspondence Rée sent from Berne included a letter from the Elmag works in Mulhouse to Peugeot informing him that an expert's examination of the damage to the 2,500 turbo-compressor showed that repairs would take between ten and twelve months as moulding patterns for these turbine blades no longer existed. A new press to create the tank bodies had been ordered from Fallersleben, which had to be brought by barge down the Canal Doubs.[34]

While the Germans' attention was on the Peugeot works, Rée sent messages by courier to André. On 9 November, the Marty piston and axle factory at Sochaux was attacked. André and two men broke in, overpowered two French guards and placed a 1-kg charge on the 500-kW transformer and 750 g on the 100-kW transformer, pulverising them. The flying pieces of metal smashed three electric motors, a switchboard, two batteries of accumulators and 1,500 litres of oil. According to Rée's report written several weeks later,

These actions completely re-established good morale in area. One of Sochaux directors, in charge of gardienage said that sabotage would continue for the rest of the war, and it could never be stopped. Germans have asked for 800 French guards for Sochaux. I repeat extreme importance of talk by Jacques Duchesse to the Gardiens de France, and of a slogan for them. It would brace boys up if mention could be made of op. on BBC. Vichy press restricts itself to reporting shootings of terrorists and burnt farms, and derailment of French passenger trains, mixing all up with the wave of revolutionary hooliganism which is sweeping the country, and which police can't stop. N.B. I am very well in with Gendarmes of region, having been introduced to all chefs, as an Alsatian who must not be molested.[35]

Written in pencil at the bottom of the note was a postscript. 'Thy 17 training is being invaluable in this area. Please thank Rheam and his staff …' and then 'P.P.S. DO YOUR BEST TO KEEP RAF AWAY!'[36]

Attempts were made to derail trains in the area and, following the instructions Rée had received at Brickendonbury, the explosives blew away a length of some ¾ metre. However, it was found that unscrewing a whole length of rail worked a lot better. As a result, seven trains were derailed at Monchanin, Millay and Luzy.[37] The l'Epée Machine Tool shop at the Leroy foundries in Ste-Suzanne were also attacked and numerous small sabotage operations undertaken including blowing up the Mont Cenis tunnel into Italy.[38]

On 19 November, an auxiliary compressor arrived at the Peugeot works and was stood in a yard covered in tarpaulin. When work finished for the evening, two workmen managed to attach a limpet bomb to it and half an hour later it blew up. The following day, three workmen climbed over the factory's perimeter wall and destroyed the 8-metre-high sand foundry. Other workmen started a 'go slow' policy; they deliberately took their time to repair the damage, replaced parts with defective ones and deliberately made faulty components. This was the kind of passive sabotage taught at Brickendonbury.[39]

However, the team's success was not to last. Following the arrest of about eighty Peugeot workers on 27 November, Rée called at the house of Monsieur Hauger, a Sochaux schoolmaster, to discover when the door opened a man standing there with a pistol pointing at him. He thought he was pretending to be a gangster but he soon made it clear he was a Feldgendarme. Ordered inside, he was told that Hauger, his mother and sister had been arrested after a Sten gun and some grenades had been found in the house. He was told that he would be taken to the gendarmerie for interrogation at six that evening. According to Rée's report,

> Since I knew that they were looking for a certain Henri, a tall, fair Englishman, in that region, and since I had 50,000 francs on me, I decided not to risk the interrogation, and after having lit a pipe, and poured out a drink for both of us, I knocked him on the head with a bottle. The blow did not have much result – he emptied his pistol – six shots. I think that four hit me, but I believe that they were blanks, because they did not injure me.
>
> We fought for half an hour, at the end of which we were both exhausted, and he let me escape. I was so weak – he had hit me several times on the head with the butt of his pistol! – that I forgot that he had my wallet in his pocket with all my identity papers, and I had not the strength to ride my bicycle. I forced myself to cross the fields (and swim across two rivers!) to a little village 3 kms. away, where I went to some friends who looked after me and sent for a doctor.[40]

With the assistance of a *passeur*, he crossed the border into Switzerland. According to the Spartacus website, this was despite him being shot in the shoulder, arm, side and lung.[41] While recovering in Porrentruy hospital, he made arrangements whereby André took over the industrial sabotage and Jean Simon, codenamed Claude, organised the attacks on the railways. Messages were sent by courier, in one of which he said, 'Thy Scotland training invaluable for crossing border.' After further treatment in Geneva, he was sent up into the mountains to convalesce. Although he stayed in Switzerland until May 1944, he was in contact with London and, through a courier, was able to send and receive messages to his teams in France.[42]

When he heard that tank production at the Peugeot works was due to restart on 8 December with the arrival of a replacement press and special springs from Fallersleben in Germany, his plan was to intercept the delivery in front of the St Quentin lock gates on the Doubs canal. According to Buckmaster, Rée was involved in the attack but it was not mentioned in his debrief.

Harry and his men were now able to devote their full time to foiling the Germans' plan, for they no longer had to report each day for work at the plant. Accordingly, the gang made their way down the canal bank, having been tipped off about the imminence of the press's arrival. The canal ran through deserted yards and behind disused sheds and shabby allotments. Harry and his men hid themselves in a large gardening shed and waited.

Shortly afterwards the barge came into sight. It was manned by a French crew and there was a guard of a few Germans on it. As it came up to them, Harry and his men opened up a murderous fire with automatic weapons and soon the barge came to a halt, swinging across the placid canal as the crew left the controls and jumped for the shore. The Germans fired back, but they were soon overpowered and the barge was in the hands of the Resistance. Harry's men boarded her, taped explosive below the waterline, on the new press and in the engine-room and quickly left before anyone could give the alarm. Within a few minutes the exploding barge herself gave the alarm. By then it was too late. The new press and the barge were useless. So was the canal, a fact which further infuriated the Germans, for it was one of their favourite ways of passing midget submarines from the Loire to the Mediterranean. Harry and his men pulled back to wait for the next move.[43]

Having gained in confidence from these sabotage operations, on 13 December a team attacked the Japy Works in Beaucourt. Two days before they were to go into production, four American turret lathes producing 90,000 fuse screws a month for the Schuster works in Vienne were destroyed. On 18 December, incendiaries destroyed the paint store, seven lorries and 800 tyres at the Koechlin Works in Belfort, and at Gy aerodrome hangars containing Wehrmacht food were burnt down causing damage of several million francs. Also that month, they attacked the Wittmer Works in Seloncourt and the Maillard works in Montbéliard, where an 800-gram charge put on the outer door to the transformers put them out of action for a month.[44]

On 9 December, Peugeot workmen sabotaged parts needed for German ambulances so that only 150 left the factory instead of 250. The following day a delivery of parts arrived from Germany and was spilled into the canal.

In early January 1944, the Peugeot works were attacked again, putting the milling machine for tank trap teeth out of action. The Krauss boring and homing machine was destroyed, which stopped cylinder production indefinitely and held up the delivery of 160 chassis. The high-precision Churchill rectifying machine, a special tank lathe for Focke-Wulf wing parts, was also destroyed. The last three machines were the only ones of their kind in the area and were irreplaceable. On 10 January, a derailment at Dampierre destroyed Wehrmacht material and caused a three-day blockage. A further attack on the Peugeot works on 12 January destroyed the transformers in the coach building. Foot stated that it halted production for three weeks.[45]

More sabotage continued. The railway works at Belfort were attacked destroying eight locomotives by placing scrap iron in the cylinders. A locomotive hydraulic jack was also destroyed, which, as it was irreparable and there was no replacement, paralysed the replacement of axles at Belfort. Locomotives therefore had to be sent elsewhere to be repaired.

On 20 January, a derailment at Voujeaucourt destroyed a locomotive and four wagons, causing a four-day stoppage. The Wittmer Works in Seloncourt were sabotaged again on 27 January causing almost total stoppage. A train was burnt out at Chagnay, a goods train derailed at Monchanin and a train carrying Germans home on leave was derailed at Millay, leaving thirty-seven dead.

On 10 February, two replacement turret lathes for Focke-Wulf part production and a compressor recently arrived from Germany for the Peugeot works were destroyed before they could be installed.[46] Buckmaster detailed the operation. According to Buckmaster, the Resistance farther up the line warned Harry and his men that the Germans had managed to find another press which they were sending under heavy guard to the factory.

'What are we going to do?' one of the gang demanded.

'We'll meet them when they arrive,' was the decisive answer. 'Send the word round that everyone's to be ready to go into hiding as soon as the shooting is over. We'll go to Claude's. Tell him to expect us. Things are likely to be pretty hot,' Claude's was a safe house where they should be able to hide-out.

On the day when the press was due at the Peugeot factory, Harry and his men were in position in a small tabac opposite the factory entrance. Three more men with sub machine guns were hidden in a yard next to the gate. The idea was that when the convoy pulled up at the gate waiting for the keeper to open up, the resisters would strike. At midday police and military motor-cyclists cordoned off the adjacent streets. Ten minutes later the tank-body press arrived on a huge truck. The whole area in front of the gate was filled with Germans, police and transport. Harry gave the signal, a grenade lobbed on to the carrier truck, and from two sides a murderous fire was unleashed on the massed Germans.

A free fight ensued. The Germans were enraged and confused and opened up indiscriminately on anything they saw. Harry and his men dodged from shop to shop, through back doors, and hammered the security forces. Bombs were lobbed from a roof on to the lorry and a small fire was started. Everyone was rushing about loosing off machine-pistols and small arms and motor-cyclists were ordered to cut off the resisters. Harry gave the order to pull out. He and his men made their getaway before the Germans became sufficiently organized to seal them off. Nevertheless they sent in hundreds of police and Gestapo agents from Besançon to the area around the factory. They arrested large numbers of workers and forced from them descriptions of the men who had absconded of the two foremen and the three auxiliary workers who had been in the factory for the weeks before the sabotage. Pictures of the foremen were posted in the streets. Drawings of the other three were alongside them.[47]

Foot reported the works being out of action for five weeks.[48] In the meantime, Rée and his men moved away from the area to avoid arrest but the sabotage continued. On 20 February, a derailment between Besançon and Montbéliard destroyed seven trucks of German war material and the following day a loading crane at the Montbéliard Canal was destroyed. In March, eleven high-tension pylons were brought down, cutting the electricity supply to the Peugeot works and on 15 March the electrically treated oven for aircraft parts, which the Germans had been waiting three months for, was destroyed within half an hour of its delivery from Fallersleben. The same treatment was given to a Hartz hydraulic press for Focke-Wulf engine cowlings which had just taken three weeks to install and adjust. With the Focke-Wulf order reduced by 60 per cent, the Germans' understandable anger and frustration led to anti-sabotage measures and threats against the Peugeot workers. The situation became so bad that they went on strike on 22 March and the Germans responded by introducing Waffen SS guards into the factories.

On 22 April, the steel railway bridge over the Haute Saône Canal, a kilometre south of Bavilliers, was brought down and on 16 May their final act of sabotage was to stop a train in broad daylight and then send it at full speed into an empty train 500 yards south of Montbéliard, which blocked the line for some time.[49]

Rée then used one of the escape lines to reach Spain on 10 May. Arrested by the Spanish police, he spent three weeks in the Miranda de Ebro prison camp before being released. Arriving in England on 7 August, he provided valuable intelligence on other inmates in Miranda, including flying-bomb technology, as well as on the individuals in his network who had helped him. He also commented on what he thought was the unhelpful attitude of Major Haslam, the British Consular official responsible for extricating British subjects. Once rested, he worked with the operational section of L'État-major des Forces Françaises de l'Intérieur (*EMFFI*).

In recognition of Rée's efforts, in June 1944 the British awarded him the Order of the British Empire and the French a Companion in the Légion d'Honneur. The following year, he was recommended for a further reward. In an unsigned citation, it stated that

Had it been necessary to rely on Allied bombing to put the [Peugeot] factory out of action, it would have required a large force of bombers at fairly frequent intervals to achieve similar disruption ... It was only after a personal visit to this area that HQ officers realised to the full the immense authority which Captain Rée wields in the Doubs and neighbouring departments, where his name is legendary, and the prestige of Great Britain at the pinnacle.[50]

In the words of one of Rée's collaborators, 'Thanks to his example the area became one hundred per cent Resistance-minded from the end of 1943, and did not rest until the expulsion of the enemy after inflicting grievous loss on them. This result, which so greatly benefited the Allied cause, is directly attributable to Captain Rée's diplomacy, steady courage, unfailing self-sacrifice and personal magnetism.'[51]

Major General Colin Gubbins, in his citation for Rée being given a further award, stated that

Captain REE organised, directed and personally led the sabotage attacks on these factories between 5 November 1943 and 3 March 1944. The attack on the centrifugal compressor in the compressor room necessitated his crawling in the dust under conditions of great danger and physical strain. The compressor was completely destroyed. In the same operation Captain REE and his men destroyed a large lathe in the heavy machinery shop.

Later he and his men attacked and destroyed a new compressor while it was standing in a lorry in the works yard. He also put out of action a jig borer, another compressor, a two-drill borer, the washing tower of the gas producer plant, the foundry sand dryers and the body work transformers, and destroyed six thousand tyres in the tyre depot. These activities were planned and co-ordinated with the Peugeot management by Captain REE who personally led the attacks and, on one occasion, only escaped under heavy small arms fire by swimming a river. He was twice wounded but escaped.

The result of these attacks was that Peugeot factories, which produced parts and aircraft components for the enemy, were made completely unproductive for five months and only started producing on a small scale in March 1944.

After a short time recovering from his wounds, Captain REE again started to direct sabotage activities in the area. His prestige and authority were enormous and his activities have become legendary. He did not cease from his work until the liberation of France.

For his outstanding gallantry, his diplomacy in getting the Peugeot management to co-operate in his sabotage activities, and for his devotion to duty over a long period, it is recommended that Captain REE be appointed a Companion in the Distinguished Service Order.[52]

The success of Rée's blackmail sabotage meant that the SOE encouraged other organisers in France and elsewhere to adopt it. After the war, Rheam commented that

We have not made enough use of managements and owners of installations who, whilst unable to do physical acts of sabotage, can be contacted and from whom technical advice can be obtained which we, in turn, can pass on to saboteurs. There should always be a gap between management and staff in matters of this nature … Make the utmost use of our 'Blackmail' methods where patriotic incentive is insufficient. Even if the Germans suspect internal sabotage, they must expand manpower to stop or keep it under control.[53]

CHAPTER 8

Learning from Experience: Insight into Industrial Sabotage by Those Involved

Given the importance of sabotage operations in the outcome of the war, those involved in the organisation and training, particularly the various Commandants at Brickendonbury, produced numerous reports, some of which would have been copied and forwarded to the heads of other sections as well as to the War Office. Some may well have been read by Churchill himself, or maybe he had one of his staff brief him on their findings.

One imagines that there was a recognition in the upper echelons of SOE that the experiences – not just of the instructors, but also of the saboteurs themselves – were worth recording, just in case there were further conflicts in which industrial sabotage might be used. There was every point in ensuring that mistakes were learned from and successes highlighted. It would be interesting to know whether the military today uses the experiences of the Brickendonbury staff and students in its planning and operations.

The first three reports, as far as I know, have never been published before and may well only have been read by those who needed to know. The last was included in Professor Michael R. D. Foot's history of the SOE in France. It was compiled by Major A. M. Brooks, Evaluations Committee, who, following the Liberation of France, visited numerous factories that had been sabotaged and generated a comprehensive list of their location, the damage and the impact. It was used to recompense those companies who had agreed to have their vital machinery sabotaged to avoid their factory from being bombed by the RAF or USAAF in what was called 'the Blackmail Sabotage Scheme'.

*

Industrial Sabotage Course

Programme Notes

This Programme is typical of one suitable for Belgian, French or British Students.

Students are required to make up and place charges on common machines. This is done before they have received any appropriate instruction and they realise, probably for the first time, that machines consist of a number of parts and that the charge cannot be placed anywhere if the machine is to be destroyed or seriously damaged.

The visit to the Iron and Steel Works is largely regarded as practical revision of common mechanical and electrical machinery.

Demolition IV comprises linking-up and initiating charges in the dark.

The visit to the Docks is largely regarded as practical revision of common machinery.

The visit to the Canal included placing charges on the lock gates.

Review of Course included general principles of Sabotage.

In the later stages of the War instruction on Passive Methods and Factories was introduced and the following included in the last week of the course.

Military Targets – 3½ hours.

Prevention of Demolitions – 2 hours.

MOST SECRET

COPY
GR/1933   24th August, 1944
To: Director of Training   From: C.C.,
S.T.S. H.Q.   S.T.S. 17.

S.O.E. TRAINING

Report on the development of Industrial Sabotage training at S.T.S. 17. With reference to your JTY/4872/A.1. dated 4th August, 1944, I enclose herewith the Report asked for in the second paragraph of your letter.

At a later date I hope to submit a further Report which will deal more fully with our methods and the reasons we have adopted them as I feel this may be of value, if, at some later date, it is necessary to re-open Industrial Sabotage Schools. In the meantime I think the present Report will meet your immediate requirements.

I have somewhat exceeded the strict limits of your terms of reference, but it has been necessary to do this in order to give a comprehensive picture of the work that has been carried out here and the difficulties that have been experienced.

I have made recommendations some of which refer to the other technical branches of the Organisation. As you know, my relations with them have not been as happy as I should have liked, but I do hope that the recommendations I have made will not be construed as criticisms of any personnel. They are not written in that spirit, but are my considered opinions as an Engineer and as a result of my experience as Commandant of what I suppose is the first School ever to have been opened for the teaching of Industrial Sabotage.

I am afraid I have not yet completed Volume III of the Handbook and this is only a part of the outstanding work that must be done before all the work that has been carried out here is on record. I am pressing forward with this as fast as possible, but it will be some little time before they are complete.

Filed in S.I.   (Signed) G. Rheam

Report On The Development Of Industrial Sabotage Training At S.T.S. 17 August 1941 – August 1944

Foreword

Resistance in the present War has been confined to the Occupied Countries and has taken two forms, Secret Armies for guerrilla warfare and sabotage groups specialising in attacks on Industry. These two kinds of attack, although complementary and to some extent overlapping, are essentially different.

In Industrialised Europe, the Secret Armies can only play their most important part in the closing stages of the War when the enemy is in retreat; it is in the earlier stages that sabotage has its greatest value.

The present War has not demonstrated the full possibilities of sabotage which did not develop on an organised basis until the middle period. In a future War, however, if properly planned sabotage can be carried out in the enemy's country immediately it begins – and this pre-supposes the existence of a Sabotage Organisation before the War starts – it will have an immediate and decisive influence on the course of events.

23.8.44

Introduction

1. This Report reviews the development of Industrial Sabotage Training at S.T.S. 17; it refers to some of the difficulties that have been experienced and makes recommendations with a view to avoiding them on a future occasion.

2. Organised sabotage was not developed in the last War and no previous experience was available on which instruction could be based. It was necessary, therefore, to start from scratch and first develop suitable methods of sabotage and then to devise a suitable training programme.

3. At this time it appeared to be the generally accepted view that Industrial Sabotage was simply a profitable sideline to the activities of secret army personnel, but it early became apparent that this was a wrong point of view and that, properly planned and carried out, sabotage might well be decisive and cause the early defeat of a country by removing its ability to produce weapons. This can be illustrated by the fact that, by attacking the Power Stations of this country, Industry could be paralysed for a very long period with less than two tons of explosive.

The Problem Training Has To Meet

4. The object of Industrial Sabotage is to stop production. This is not a demolition problem and an Agent must have more than just a knowledge of explosives.

Modern Industry is very complex and has been built up over a long period by engineers. Always precautions are taken in the building and equipping of Factories to ensure that the breakdown of one or two machines will not cause a material reduction in output. Since the start of the War, many additional precautions have been taken to prevent, as far as possible, loss of production in the event of damage by air raids.

It is, therefore, quite impossible for the haphazard destruction of machinery to cause any worthwhile loss of production.

5. If the result is to be decisive, the problem must be tackled from the same point of view as that which has brought Industry to its present pitch of efficiency, that is, from an engineering point of view.

Once this was realised, there were no great difficulties in developing suitable methods of sabotage and training programme followed naturally. What was more difficult was to make this programme suitable for non-technical personnel. Of the 880 students trained up to the beginning of August, 1944, less than 5 per cent have had any technical experience of Industry.

6. From a training point of view, the problem may be divided into six parts:

(i) To know which are the Industries important to the enemy's War effort.

(ii) To know which are the vital parts of these Industries.

(iii) To be able to locate these vital parts.

(iv) To be able to recognise the vital machinery.

(v) To know how to destroy this machinery.

(vi) To know how to use explosives.

Of these, (iv) is much the most difficult for non-technical personnel to learn and as experience was gained, more and more attention was paid to this aspect of the problem.

Technical Training

7. It is considered that the lines on which the training was developed are satisfactory and the results obtained by the Basic Course were, on the

whole, surprisingly good. Each course was divided into groups of not more than 12 students and each group was instructed separately.

(A) Courses

Three types of Courses were provided:-

(i) Basic Course

This was designed for non-technical personnel and lasted three weeks. It reviewed the organisation of Industry and dealt with the sabotage (active and passive) of common machinery, electric power, transport, communications and Works & Factories of different sorts. When required, it included shipping and canals. The syllabus was varied in accordance with the nationality of the student and it included about ten visits to Works of one kind or another. A typical programme for a French or Belgian party is attached as Appendix B.

In the Autumn of 1943 much of the instruction on passive methods of sabotage was cut out and instructions on targets of a military nature were introduced.

(ii) Specialist Courses

These courses were begun at the request of Country Sections for Agents who were going to specialise in one particular branch of Industry or who were going out on a special mission. They usually lasted from one to seven days.

(iii) Operational Courses

These were designed for 'coup de main' and 'Combined Operation' parties, and were concerned only with the party's immediate objective. They usually lasted from two to seven days.

8. It will be appreciated that to cover such a wide range of subjects in the Basic Course – a range of subjects that normally takes engineers years to learn – presented a problem of singular difficulty. Satisfactory results, however, obtained:

(i) By reducing the instructions to fundamental principles, which were in turn based on,

(ii) The time it takes to repair or replace a machine.

(iii) By concentrating on recognition features rather than on how and why a machine works.

(iv) Standardisation and

(v) The elimination of unnecessary alternatives (One paper on the sabotage of aeroplanes, issued by the Organisation, contained no fewer than twenty-three methods of attack. No student can remember such a list, which only confuses him.)

9. One serious fault was the short time allowed on the Basic Course and on a future occasion, to make the training thorough, it should be increased to five weeks' duration, the last being devoted to additional practical work and schemes. It is felt that this extension of time is essential (*). Thoroughly trained men will always produce better results than a larger number of semi-trained, and as in the Field an Agent trained in this Country has considerable influence and is looked upon as an expert, it is important that he does not undermine confidence in the Organisation by making a mistake.

10. The Basic Course entails a very intensive effort on the part of the Student. On a course longer than three weeks, leave will be necessary and it is recommended that weekend leave is granted each Saturday from 1600 hours (see also section 39).

11. With non-technical personnel, Specialist Courses are not satisfactory unless the Agent has first passed through the Basic Course. They give him an incomplete training without any proper foundation and fit him, not altogether adequately, only for his one particular mission.

(i) Most Army technical courses last three months or more although the student is specially selected on account of mechanical aptitude.

It is strongly recommended that every agent should pass through the Basic Course, and that the Specialist Course should be regarded as refresher courses in a particular subject or an extension of the Basic Course if the Agent is concerned with an industry not included in that Course. Under no circumstances should they be recorded as a means of reducing the period of training to be undergone by the Agent.

12. Operational Courses present no difficulties. The instruction should include a visit to a Works of the same type and size as the target.

This gives the Party greatly increased confidence and enables them to appreciate any special recognition feature and the size of the machinery, a subject non-technical personnel are very liable to underestimate. Practice attacks on this same plant should be arranged, whatever the security difficulties.

13. It was found that it was much easier to teach active methods of sabotage, that is, methods involving the use of explosives, than passive. Passive methods in general require more technical knowledge, and any but the most simple are not suitable for non-technical personnel unless their training can be extended over a longer period.

14. The programme was so arranged that the Basic Course of three weeks' duration occurred every four weeks; this gave a 'free week' between Courses, and enabled Operational and Specialist Courses to be concentrated in this period. Owing to the shortage of instructional staff, it proved inconvenient to have Basic and Specialist Courses running concurrently.

(B) Visits

15. Visits to Works and Factories and similar installations form an invaluable aid in training which any amount of lectures cannot replace. As many as possible should be included in a Course. It was found most satisfactory to commence with simple visits such as Pumping Stations, where a variety of common machinery can be seen, and to finish with the larger engineering factories. Plants of the latter type tend to overwhelm the student and should be left until he has become more machine minded. This conforms to the natural sequence of instruction, and is no disadvantage.

16. Although it is best to take the student to installations of the type he is likely to find in his area in the Field, this is not essential. His need at this time is to obtain as much practice in the recognition of machinery as possible and any plant containing a representative selection of common machinery will make a good visit since such machinery is found in all types of Industry.

17. The Basic Course visits were regular features of the training programme. The necessary arrangements were made with a Director of the Firm and the same Instructor was sent on each occasion. In this way, very happy relations were soon established with the Firms and in some cases the Party was allowed to go round the Works without a guide. This is the best arrangement as the Instructor can talk more freely.

Except in the case of Docks and similar installations, a party visiting a Works should not exceed twelve in number and where possible there should be two Instructors, one for each six students. If this is not done, it is quite impossible for the majority of students to understand what is going on.

18.   Visits for Special Course were specially arranged either through the Ministry concerned or through the Security Branch of the Organisation.

19. With one possible exception, the management of all the many forms visited have done everything possible to help and nothing has been too much trouble. There is no doubt that this willing cooperation has contributed to the success of the training.

(C) Exercises

20. It was realised during 1942 that the Basic Course did not include enough practical work, but it was not until the beginning of 1943 that Security Regulations permitted practice attacks on actual installations. These were started in January 1943 and became of very high value.

The first type of exercise introduced as the night attack in which the students were 'dropped' about a mile from their objective; they then had to make their way to the target which was guarded by sentries, gain access to it and place the charges on what they considered was the vital machinery.

The approach to the target is of value if the students can be accompanied by an Instructor – this was not always possible.

21. Too many night schemes were found to interfere with the efficiency of the students owing to lack of sleep, but in view of the need to include still

more practical work, daylight exercises were introduced, in addition, at a later date. In these, the students were taken to the entrance to the target building, from which point the exercise was carried out as an operation.

These exercises although carried out in daylight proved of great value and they should certainly be included as an addition to the night schemes in any syllabus of training.

22. As a general rule, the students should be divided up into parties of not more than four for both the night schemes and the daylight exercises; this ensures that every man has a real 'job' to do and it is more representative of actual conditions in the Field than if the whole group of twelve does the exercise at the same time. It means that the exercise has to be repeated three times in the one night, but the benefits obtained are worthwhile.

23. Pumping Stations, Power Stations and Locomotive Sheds (night only) are typical of the good targets for these exercises. It is not recommended that factories should be attacked as it is difficult to obtain representative conditions and the practical and security problems involved are considerable.

24. Sabotage Students should be taught towncraft in addition to fieldcraft, and how to move about buildings which are occupied. There was not time to include this in the training at S.T.S. 17, but it is important.

25. On no account should either a night scheme or daylight exercise be allowed to become a test of the Firm's Security Organisation. If this is permitted and the exercise is successful, someone will get a rap from the management or the Security Officer. This will interfere with the good relations that must be built up, not only with the management, but with the junior officials and workpeople as well.

(D) Instructors
26. Until recently the whole of the technical instructions at S.T.S. 17 was carried out by myself and three assistant instructors. Concurrently,

suitable methods of sabotage had to be worked out and a training system devised; in addition, handbooks and demolition reports had to be prepared.

This has proved too much and, almost from the beginning, the School has been understaffed. Any future establishment must allow for a larger staff.

The fault was due partly to failure, at the beginning to minimalise the problem on broad enough lines, but ultimately to the impossibility of obtaining suitable personnel, either from Army or Civilian sources.

One result of this has been that the original key Instructors have had no change of employment or chance of advancement and have seen members of the technical and other branches of the Organisation promoted more rapidly. This has been a source of genuine grievance as they are experienced engineers and have proved themselves first-class instructors. Future War Establishments should take into consideration the need for the promotion of Instructors.

Some men, too, are certain to find instructing irksome after a time and to desire more active employment. But their experience is needed by the Organisation and posts in other Sections should be open to all Instructors. Their technical qualifications, experience and knowledge of the student particularly for posts as Technical Advisers to Army G.H.Q.s and Missions abroad.

27. The teaching of such large technical subjects as Industrial Sabotage to non-technical personnel in a period of a few weeks is a difficult problem and special attention should be given to the selection of the Instructors.

It is suggested that the following qualifications are necessary; they are given in order of importance:-

(i) Not less than eight–ten years' general experience in one or more of the Heavy Industries (or their equivalent, e.g. Power Stations). A shorter period may be accepted for Junior Instructors working under supervision.

(ii) Considerable practical experience of machinery. This means that men who have spent most of their lives in design and sales offices will probably not be suitable. Experience in the erection of heavy machinery or in the Works Engineer's Department of a large Firm should be of particular advantage.

(iii) A degree or at least a diploma from a Technical College.

(iv) Military experience. When a potential instructor has not got this training, he should pass through the paramilitary courses of the Organisation before being posted to an Industrial Sabotage School.

In short, the type of Instructor required is an Engineer who has plenty of practical experience and has a wide knowledge of the various types of machinery found in Industry, preferably to the point of view of both the manufacturer and the user; men from the teaching staff of Technical Colleges, from the Offices of Consulting Engineers and from the Sales side of Industry are unlikely to be suitable unless they have some considerable practical experience. Teaching experience is not needed; none of the Instructors at S.T.S. 17 had previously lectured.

EQUIPMENT

28. The School, or such Schools if there is more than one, should be provided with the following equipment:-

(i) An epidiascope of the Aldis type for each group of twelve students (the smaller Newton type is not suitable).

(ii) Lantern Slides and Photographs of all common types of machines and machine tools (photographed alone and as part of an installation). These should be selected to show the recognition features, and should preferably show equipment of Continental manufacture.

(iii) A good quality camera for photographing demolition.

(iv) A 16-mm Cine Projector with sound, together with suitable films showing Industrial processes.

(v) Simplified coloured diagrams of Industrial processes and machines.

(vi) Models of up-to-date common machinery and Continental locomotives. The machine models should preferably be sectioned.

(vii) Telephone line equipment.

(viii) Samples of common machines. These should be of medium size, preferably of Continental make. They may be second-hand but should not be obsolete. They should be properly installed and, when possible, provisions should be made for running them 'light'. A list of the machines which it will be desirable to have is given in Appendix A.

(ix) Samples of Enemy equipment – Aeroplanes, Guns, Tanks etc., also of Continental railway wagons.

(x) Regular supplies of machinery and steelwork for demolition purposes and of flat bottomed rail track.

(xi) Lifting Tackle etc. of capacities up to 10 tons, together with all necessary accessory equipment.

(xii) A small workshop, including lathe, drill and screwing machine.

LIST OF TECHNICAL TERMS

29. Although every endeavour was made to reduce to a minimum technical terms, the use of many was unavoidable.

It is very desirable that Students should have such terms correctly translated into their own language. This was not possible at S.T.S. 17 as there was no Interpreter available with the necessary technical knowledge.

Such lists should be prepared on another occasion and preferably separate lists should be made for each group of lectures, i.e. one list for Common Machinery, another for Electrical Machinery, another for Transport and so on.

MIXING OF STUDENTS OF DIFFERENT NATIONALITIES.

30. S.T.S. 17 was one of the few Schools at which Students of different nationalities were instructed together. Although sometimes presenting small difficulties in training, for example, on one occasion it was necessary to have three different Interpreters translating at the same time for one group of twelve students, on the whole, it proved an unqualified success. It gave Students an opportunity of getting to know men of other nationalities and helped in a small way to promote good feelings between nations. British students were trained in exactly the same way as Allied.

LOCATION OF SCHOOLS

31. Schools for Industrial Sabotage should be located within easy reach of an Industrial area, preferably an area containing Basic Industries and

large Docks, but in the open country to avoid undesirable attention and provide facilities for demolition training. It is an advantage if they can be near Headquarters and the other Technical Stations.

Hertford has met these conditions remarkably well and only two of the regular visits were outside a 30-mile radius. This is important as travelling time on visits must be cut down to a minimum to avoid waste of instructional time.

DEMOLITION TRAINING

32. Demolition training as it was first introduced into the organisation centred around the explosive and what it could be made to do. Instructors, in their enthusiasm, tended to multiply the ways in which the same things could be done and devised all sorts of interesting, but hardly practical, experiments.

33. This is the wrong approach to the problem. The training must have in mind the ultimate Target – Industry, that is, Machinery. It must be suited to, not 'Sappers' or the Agent trained in this Country, but the Operator in the Field who in the majority of cases will have received only a few hours' instruction under unfavourable conditions and who has probably never witnessed a practical demonstration.

Unless these points are constantly borne in mind, training may easily develop on the wrong lines, particularly in the preliminary Schools where 'make-believe' targets have to be used.

The training should be:-

(i) As simple as possible – if there is more than one method of doing a thing, only one, that which is most foolproof *in the dark* should be taught.

(ii) Standardised throughout all the schools of the Organisation.

(iii) Based on the use of standard made-up charges and *what they will do* against the different materials used in the construction of machines.

Nothing should be taught about explosives as such, all that is needed is that the Agent should know what a standard charge will do; how it should be initiated and how it can be connected up with other charges. Any further information is unnecessary, will be confused when it is passed on to others and will lead to errors; but the manipulation of the charge, leads and initiators must be practised until it becomes a habit which will never be forgotten.

34. A simplified and standardised system of training was introduced in all the Schools in this country last summer and as a result the standard reached by the Students in Demolitions has greatly improved.

It is recommended that all demolition Instructors should pass through the Basic Sabotage Course before commencing their instruction duties. In this way they can gain a good general picture of the Target the student is being trained to attack and it enables them better to appreciate the problems involved. This has been the practice since mid-1943.

DEMOLITION STORES
35. The standard made-up charge (1½ lb and 3 lb) is the largest single factor contributing to successful demolitions in the Field. It is desired to place this on record as there was considerable opposition to its introduction, which was delayed in consequence. It has been pointed out earlier in this report that what is suitable for the scientist or the trained 'Sapper' may be quite unsuitable for the Operator in the Field, and it is from his point of view that these problems must be regarded. Experience has shown that the ordinary Operator cannot make up charges correctly every time and that he develops unsound ideas on what is required unless shapes and sizes are laid down. Of equal importance is the lack of time and opportunity to carry out such work in safety, if large quantities of explosives are involved.

36. The other stores in use at present are generally satisfactory, but for record purposes it may be worthwhile to list improvements or additional items that will be of immediate benefit:-
(i) Standard 1½-lb and 3-lb charges with provision for self-contained time delay and initiating device (the less the Operator has to do, the more chance is there that the demolition will be successful). The charge must remain flexible.
(ii) An Adhesive to enable standard charges to be fixed in position without the use of magnets, adhesive tape or string etc.

(iii) A 'Time Pencil' more accurate and less dependent on temperature.

(iv) An Anti-removal Fuse (air-armed) smaller in size than the present store and therefore of more universal application.

(v) A Detonator which cannot be inserted into a Time Pencil or Fog Signal etc. the wrong way round.

(vi) A general-purpose incendiary suitable for igniting transformers and heavier oils.

(vii) All stores, Cordtex, Adhesive Tape, Time Pencils etc. should be finished matt, dark grey or other suitable colour.

(viii) A method of sabotaging a railway wagon axle-box so that it will still run hot after not less than 100 miles but before the mileage reaches 300.

(ix) A simple but certain method for causing train derailments.

37. It is further recommended that no new stores should be put into production until they have been tried out by Students in the Training Schools under operational conditions. A device which may be perfectly satisfactory when used by Scientists and expert personnel may prove a complete failure when used by the comparatively untrained Operator.

38. It is also recommended that the Training Section should be consulted before it is decided what stores should be sent to the Field and in what proportions they should be loaded in the containers. Collectively, the Schools have more experience of what is required than any other branch of the Organisation.

SECURITY

39. It is considered that it will be in the best interests of security, if students are restricted to the School compound during the week and given leave each weekend (see section 10). This leave should be spent less than 10 miles away from the School.

RELATIONS WITH TECHNICAL SECTIONS

40. This matter is important because, unless the technical advice and the instructions given to the Country Section and the Agent is the best

and is consistent and suited to the Operators that have to be employed, satisfactory results cannot be expected. In the end it is the instructions given to the Agent which will determine whether what is accomplished by the Organisation is decisive or merely of nuisance value.

41. Quite important difficulties have occurred during the past three years between S.T.S. 17 and the other technical sections in this connection.

At the time S.T.S. was transformed into an Industrial Sabotage School, the position as far as it affected the school, was roughly as follows:-

'L' Section – collected technical intelligence, advised on methods of sabotage and issued to Country Sections and Missions Abroad instructional handbooks and pamphlets.

Station IX – advised on charges and methods of sabotage, also issued 'Contributions' (Laboratory) on sabotage methods.

Station XII – manufactured charges either in accordance with instructions from Sta. IX or in accordance with what they considered was best for the operation in question.

The personnel of these sections were, in general not recruited from the Engineering Industry and consequently they had no recent practical experience of machinery and were not aware of the modern possibilities of 'repair and replacement'. In many cases, they were not familiar with machines of the type for which they were issuing sabotage instructions. They were further handicapped by having no contact with the students and on that account were unaware of the capabilities of the Operators and the conditions likely to arise in the Field. This resulted in inconsistent, often unsound or unsuitable advice being given to the Agents and unsatisfactory stores being sent into the Field (in this connection I desire to record that when the branch of 'L' Section chiefly concerned became aware of the methods taught at S.T.S. 17 they co-operated fully).

42. To avoid corresponding difficulties on a future occasion, it is suggested that the Technical Section should be organised on the lines shown in the table opposite and as explained below, and that the personnel should have the qualifications stated:-

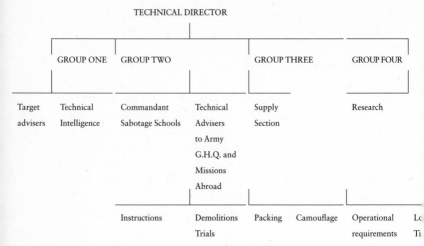

Technical Director – In charge of all technical Branches, to be a man with wide experience of Industry with at least some years of practical experience with machinery.

Group One – Corresponding to the present 'L' Section. This should comprise two sections, the first to coordinate and advise on Targets, the second to be responsible for collecting all necessary technical intelligence and for the preparation of information required by other technical branches. They should NOT issue Sabotage handbooks.

The personnel of the first section should have a wide experience of Industry but need not be practical engineers; the staff of the second should be engineers with some practical experience.

Group Two – Corresponding to the present S.T.S. 17, but including the Technical Advisers to Army G.H.Q. Missions Abroad etc.

The Commandant should be in charge of all instructions for the carrying out of demolitions trials on machinery; also for the preparation of all handbooks, pamphlets etc. on sabotage methods.

This will ensure that the instruction is kept up-to-date and is verified by actual test, and that the advice given to Missions Abroad & Country Sections agree with the instruction given to the Student.

Technical information and intelligence that he may require should be supplied by the Intelligence Branch of Group One.

The Schools should be under the Director of Training for administration and all matters other than those relating to the technical side.

The Technical Advisers should be drawn from the Instructors in the Schools or, when this is not possible, should have been through the Basic Course. This will ensure that the best advice is given to Army G.H.Q.s and the Missions Abroad. It will prevent instructing becoming a dead-end occupation and will give Instructors a chance of promotion.

The qualifications of the personnel in the whole of this Group should be as laid down on page ten of the Instructions.

Group Three – This group should be generally similar to the present Supply Section, but should have a closer liaison with the Training Schools. It should include the Packing and Camouflage Sections as these three sections should work in the closest cooperation. The key personnel should have had experience in this branch of work in civil life or in the R.A.C.C.

Group Four – Should comprise a small research Section divided into two branches; the first, if necessary in conjunction with research laboratories of civilian firms, should be concerned with the improvement of existing devices or the production of new devices required by the Operational and training Groups. The second section should deal with long-term research in the development of new devices and new methods (chemical) of sabotage.

The group should be staffed by scientists, preferably with Industrial experience.

The grouping of all the technical sections under one Director should do much to eliminate inter-departmental friction and to ensure that all branches work together as a team to produce the best possible Sabotage Organisation.

Relations With Country Sections

43. Close relations with Country sections are of mutual benefit.

Periodical visits by Country Section Heads and their senior Officers should be encouraged. In this way, they will keep in touch with latest training methods and the Schools with the problems of the Section. Liaison of this kind keeps the Instructors au fait with what is going on and helps to maintain their interest in the Organisation as a whole.

It is recommended that at least the junior Officers in Country Sections should go through the Basic Sabotage Course before taking up their duties in their offices. In this they will know something of the capabilities of their Agents and the target which they have to attack.

It is a help to the School to have some knowledge of the Student's ultimate mission and informal interviews with these agents who have returned from the Field and have dealt with sabotage matters are of great value. Experience has shown that over a tankard of beer many more details of interest can be extricated from an Agent, than can be obtained at the more formal interview in London.

Airborne Troops

44. Although, properly, outside the scope of this report, attention is drawn to the fact that airborne and other troops used against Industrial Targets should be given technical training on the lines developed by this Organisation.

G. Rheam, B.Sc. A.C.C.I. Lt.Col. R.E.M.F.

Commandant S.T.S. 17

Appendix A

1. Representative Types Of Common Machinery

	Minimum Size
1. Low Pressure Centrifugal Pump	12-inch–18-inch suction
2. High Pressure Centrifugal Pump	6 to 8 stage – 6-inch suction.

3. Single Stage Blower
4. Roots Blower
5. Eccentric Vane (Beale) Blower

6. Vertical Triple Expansion Steam Engine	100 hp
7. Horizontal Compound Steam Engine	100 hp
8. 6-cyl. Diesel-Generator Set (D.C)	75 Kw.
9. High- or Low-Pressure Horizontal Reciprocating Pump	200 gpm
10. 2-Stage Vertical Compressor	400 cu. feet/min.
11. Horizontal Reciprocating Compressor	-do-
12. Rotary Convertor	250 Kw.
13. Motor Generator Set AC/DC	400 Kw.
14. 3-Ph. Transformer 500 K.V.A.	
15. Electric Winch	60 hp
16. Electric Motors, AC and DC	5 hp

Note: Some of the above types of machines may become obsolete during the next 10 to 20 years.[1]

2. EVALUATIONS *Industrial Sabotage (memorandum)*

Industrial Sabotage
(A) General Considerations

(i) Industrial sabotage was developed as a new weapon of war after the occupation of highly-industrialised countries by the Germans in 1940. After a long preparatory period during which sabotage organisers were trained and infiltrated, and during which they built up their teams inside Occupied Europe, a coordinated plan of sabotage was carried out against selected enemy industrial installations and communications. This paper summarises some of the results that were obtained in areas where a coordinated sabotage effort was made. The results achieved were highly damaging to the enemy's industrial economy in occupied countries, and were an important factor contributing to his ultimate defeat. Even greater results could have been achieved with earlier planning if the possibilities of the weapon had been foreseen.

(ii) Industrial Sabotage is a weapon that can be compared with highly accurate bombing, but it is far less costly and can be more effective. In some cases it is the only means whereby an enemy's industrial machine can be attacked. This is likely to be a factor of increasing importance with the development of underground plant designed to be impervious to bombing.

(iii) It is a clandestine activity carried out by small parties of trained operators. Though the best results can be obtained in areas where the mass of sentiment is anti-enemy, this is not an absolutely necessary prerequisite for success, and vital damage can be inflicted by trained teams even in hostile areas. A weight of pro-Allied sympathy is necessary, however, for passive sabotage to be effective.

(iv) Training is necessary to enable results to be obtained by the correct placing of small charges on vital machinery or equipment. Haphazard demolitions are practically worthless. Training in sabotage is based essentially on the principle that, to be able to achieve effective damage with small parties using concealable stores, it is necessary to acquire a knowledge of the complex structure of industry, and to be able to identify the bottleneck in particular industries. To give an example, in England at the present time an attack on three Gleeson cutters in a small factory in the London area would have a most serious effect on car production throughout the country, as all the crown wheels made for rear axles for all British manufacturers are made in this one factory. Only one man and 4½ lbs of explosive would be needed.

There are, of course, certain 'standard' bottlenecks common to the whole of the industrial set-up, notably electric power and rail communications.

Training in the use of explosives, incendiaries and devices is comparatively simple. One of the major problems for non-technical trainees is the recognition of vital machinery.

(v) A knowledge of the possibilities of sabotage is essential to the authorities responsible for defence policy. Sabotage, if properly planned and carried out, can reduce a country's war potential to the point where it becomes impossible for it to wage war.

(vi) Scientific and technical developments render the war potential of a country all the more vulnerable to sabotage. As a defensive weapon, sabotage may in the future be used in areas likely to be overrun by an enemy. As an offensive weapon, it is capable of inflicting such damage that an enemy cannot continue a struggle. And in security planning, our own vulnerability to sabotage methods cannot be overlooked.

(B) Results of Sabotage in the Last War.

The following is a summary of the results obtained by clandestine sabotage teams working in France, Belgium and Norway during the last war. The lists and accounts are not comprehensive, but they will serve to show in general what was achieved. It should be borne in mind that the sum total of effectiveness of these methods would have been even greater if the experience gained had been available earlier and if the importance of the weapon could have been foreseen. Most attacks took place in late 1943 and 1944.

From the following lists, one example in each case is given, as being illustrative of the number of men involved in the attack, the weight of explosive used and the resulting loss in production to the enemy.

This statement includes only those attacks which have been investigated since the Liberation. In many other cases it is known that successful attacks were made, but owing to the disappearance of the saboteurs and the resumption of normal work in factories, full details are not available.

1. FRANCE

Objectives attacked:
(i) 30 Hydro-electric Power Stations.
(ii) 16 High-tension substations.
(iii) Coordinated attacks on electrified railway substations and H.T. lines supplying them. Particularly from D-Day onwards, all H.T. lines came under attack, and very few lines remained in operation.
(iv) 16 factories engaged on aircraft production.
(v) 6 factories in the motor industry.
(vi) 8 factories producing electrical and radio equipment.
(vii) 4 coal mines.
(viii) 4 rubber factories.
(ix) 27 plants engaged on steel, aluminium and engineering production.

(x) 12 plants in the chemical, liquid oxygen and synthetic fuel industry.

(xi) 7 ball-bearing factories.

(xii) 3 factories in the Precision and Optical Industry.

(xiii) Communications

(a) Waterways: 19 rivers or canals blocked for periods longer than 25 consecutive days.

(b) Railways: Between June 1943 and May 1944, 1822 locomotives sabotaged.

10,500 goods trucks damaged.

After D-Day, 820 locomotives sabotages.

6–27 June, 1944, 3,000 confirmed cuts in rails, some resulting in derailments.

Appendices A and B give reports made by an investigating team on two attacks included in the list above.

(i) Etablissements Baume et Marpent, Jeumont, Nord.

(ii) Ratier Propellor Works, Figeac.

2. BELGIUM

The main effort of Belgian sabotage teams was directed against rail and inland waterway communications. At one period, January 1944, two men had achieved the stoppage of traffic on all canals and rivers connecting Belgium and France, thus forcing the enemy to make increased use of sea routes, which was exactly in line with the wishes of the Navy.

Summary of Targets Attacked:

(i) Power Stations and substations.

10 attacks.

(ii) Aircraft factories.

1 attack.

(iii) One Blast Furnace destroyed.

(iv) One Liquid Oxygen Plant and 2 Synthetic Oil Plants put out of production.

(v) Communications:

60 attacks on lock gates.

734 rail cuts.

67 derailments.

114 locomotives damaged.

(vi) Records:

5 simultaneous attacks on records of personnel listed for forced labour in the Office National du Travail, in five different towns.

(vii) Counter-scorch.

(viii) Most valuable assistance was rendered to the advancing Allied armies by teams organised by one man trained in England for this specific task. These tasks neutralised enemy demolition parties, seized control of the port area, removed the charges and held the area until the arrival of the Allied forces. The vital tidal lock gates of KRUISHEN, ROYERS, KATTENDIJCK, BONEPARTE and the S. Lock were preserved, as well as the majority of the quays and the equipment on them.

Examples of Individual Attacks:

(i) Blockage of the Canal de l'Espierres.

In August 1943, two men attacked eight steel barges with limpets and sank them at selected spots in the canal.

The result of the attack was a complete blockage of the waterway which lasted for three months.

(ii) Attack on the Espierres Lock on the Escaut.

In September 1943, two men attacked the gates on this lock. The lock was 20 m wide and was provided with three gates, 15 m high. Each leaf weighed about 18 tons. The gates were of steel, single skin construction. Channel-iron stiffeners were fixed to the low-water side.

Two limpets were used on each leaf, both near the heel post, one being as near to the pintle as possible, and the other 1 m 50 below the water level. The latter charges were placed with the limpet placing rod, and for the former the rod plus a length of rope was used. A covering party of four men held up the civilian guard while charges were being placed.

In addition, three electric motors in the operating cabin were destroyed, one by a limpet and the two others by ¾-lb charges.

The interruption of traffic resulting from this operation lasted 4½ months.

Appendix C gives a list of fifty-five canal and river sabotage attacks carried out by a small group operating in the Hainault West sector. Most of these were short-term attacks. These lists were supplied by the Regional Director of the Belgian Canal Service.

3. NORWAY

Although Norway was not a highly industrialised country, its industrial potential was considerable. The Germans planned to develop it for war-production purposes, making use of the available sources of cheap electrical power, and of its mineral resources. Sabotage teams did valuable work in limiting the value of occupied Norway to the enemy. The following are typical of operations carried out in Norway:-

(i) Orkla Pyrites Mine.

Three men attacked the convertor and transformer station on 4 May 1942, and reduced the output for a period of six months. A better result still would have been achieved but for the chance availability of spare equipment.

The transport of ore was crippled by three further attacks on locomotives in 1943 and in May and June 1944.

(ii) Glemfjord Power Station.

This supplied power to a neighbouring aluminium works. Twelve men attacked the pipeline and generators on 20 September 1942. Aluminium production was abandoned.

(iii) Stord Pyrites Mine.

A small mixed force attacked on 20 January, 1943 and severely reduced the output, which had been 12,000 tons. Production had only recovered to the 4,000 level by 1945.

(iv) Arendal Smelteverk

This source of silicon carbide was attacked by three men on 21 November 1943. Transformers were destroyed and the works were at a standstill for six months.

(v) Communications.

(a) Shipping.

Nine ships totalling 25,000 tons were sunk by limpets. This figure includes a 1,000 destroyer, sunk by an explosive charge, during launching.

(b) Railways.

During the period December 1944–April 1945, over 100 attacks were made on tracks, ranging from individual cuts to demolition of long sectors. Twenty bridges were damaged or demolished. One tunnel was blocked. Delays in troop movements were the object. Stoppage in traffic varied from six hours to twenty-one days.

(vi) Fuel and Oil.

Thirty separate attacks were made against dumps and storage tanks containing petrol, diesel, lubricating and special oils.

(vii) Atomic Weapons.

Operations carried out against the Heavy Water Plant at Norsk Hydro-Electric, and against stocks of heavy water, remain classics of sabotage. Intelligence has shown that the Germans had asked the Norsk Hydro to increase the output of heavy water to 10,000 lbs in 1942. Contact was made with the works, and the way prepared for a sabotage coup. A Combined Ops Raid failed, both bombers and gliders crashing, and the only result was an intensifying of the defensive measures. On 16 February 1943, six saboteurs, intensively trained for the objective, were dropped nearby. They carried three complete sets of charges, each capable of destroying the high-concentration cells. They attacked successfully, and destroyed the concentrating plant and 3,000 lbs of heavy water. The weight of the explosives was 11 lbs.

A raid nine months later by 174 bombers dropping 435 tons of bombs destroyed only a further 120 lbs of heavy water and failed to damage the plant.

Subsequent reports showed that the remaining stock and certain pieces of plant were to be moved to Hamburg. Stringent security measures surrounded this move, but two saboteurs were able to get aboard the ferry steamer taking the special train across Lake Tinnsjø, and placed a delayed-action charge inside the ship, sinking it in 300 fathoms, with its valuable cargo. This action ended the story of heavy water production in Norway.

The attacks are noteworthy as being illustrative of what can be achieved by trained men against important installations even when most strongly defended, and against which other forms of attack have failed.

Appendix C

Sabotage Of Canals: Hainault (West)

1. The attached list of sabotage attacks (reference EGC/HS/1285) against navigable waterways in Western Hainault was supplied by Monsieur DRAILY, regional director of the Canal service.

2. It is accompanied by
(i) Interrogator's notes, reference EGC/GB/1285A,
(ii) A map, scale 1:1,000,000 prepared by M. Draily summarising much of the information (one copy only available),
(iii) Photographs showing the results of two of the attacks (one set only available). These photographs are official ones taken by M. Draily's department during inspection and repair of the damage.

3. In studying this list the usual GSGS 4336 (1:1,000,000) map can be supplemented by the special 1:1,000,000 canal map of Belgium sent to the Evaluation Committee on 12 June 1945 by Lt. Col. Cox. This map gives profiles of the canals and other useful information: it does not show aqueducts, but these can usually be located on the GSGS maps (for a note on aqueducts see EGC/GB/1291, para. 10).

4. M. Draily was a member of the Group G (Chef de Material for Region III) but in his official capacity retained the confidence of the Germans until the end. He contributed considerably to the effects of canal sabotage both by advising on attacks beforehand and by the inefficient conduct of repairs afterwards. One of the most effective methods of delaying repairs was to undergo sudden changes of mind as to the priorities of various repairs; for example switching men from a half-finished repair to deal with the effects of a new attack elsewhere, so that in the meantime seepage of water would to some extent neutralise the half-finished repairs on the first site.

5. It is understood that a considerable amount of information similar to that in M. Draily's list but for other parts of Belgium is available in the Ministère des Travaux Publics, but time has not been available for its investigation.

HAINAULT REGION (WEST): Acts of Sabotage against navigable waterways.

Note: The following abbreviations are used

RH	Right hand
LH	Left hand
U	Upstream
D	Downstream
G	Group 'G'
AB	Armée Blanche
PA	Partisans Armée
CF25	Chemin de fer (independent railway group working in conjunction with Group 'G'

No.	Location of installation	Nature of damage	Dates of interruption – resumption of traffic	Done by
		A/. River DENDRE		
1	Lessines lock	RH leaf of D gate destroyed	10.11.42 – 21.11.42	
2	Deux-Acran lock	RH leaf of D gate damaged	23.11.42 – 9.12.42	
3	Papignies lock	LH leaf of U gate damaged	6.2.43 – 9.2.43	
4	Lessines lock	LH leaf of U gate damaged	6.2.43 – 15.2.43	
5	Rebaix lock	RH leaf of spare gate damaged	1.3.43	
6	Dam at old Lessines lock	5 beams damaged	28.3.43 – 31.3.43	
7	Rebaix lock	U gate and LH leaf of D gate destroyed. Masonry heaviy damaged.	10.4.43 – 6.5.43	
8	Papignies lock	U gate destroyed. Masonry badly damaged.	7.5.43 – 20.5.43	
9	Papignies lock	Contractor's pontoon sunk	8.5.43	
10	Rebaix lock	RH leaf of U gate destroyed	20.6.43 – 29.6.43	
11	Bilbée lock, Ath	LH leaf of U gate damaged	29..8.43 – 9.9.43	G
12	Bilbée lock, Ath	D gate destroyed. 15 m. Of lock wall destroyed	26.9.43 – 30.12.43	G

13	Lessines lock	D gate destroyed. 20 m. Of lock wall destroyed	18.12.43 – 24.2.44	G
14	Idegem lock	U gate destroyed	15.1.44 – 12.2.44	
15	Lessines lock	Coffer-dam damaged (destruction of 4 sheet piles)	9.2.44	
		B/. BLATON – ATH Canal		
16	Lock 18, Ath	RH leaf of U gate destroyed	14.5.43 – 2.6.43	G
17	Aqueduct des trois fontaines, Chievres	Vault and walls of culvert demolished	3.8.43 – 30.8.43	G
18	Lock 10, Stambruges	LH leaf upstream destroyed	25.9.43 – 14.11.43	G
19	Lock 11, Belceil	LH leaf upstream destroyed. Masonry damaged (hollow quoin and sill)	6.12.43 – 15.3.44	G
20	Lock 11, Belceil	Emergency dam (wooden beams) destroyed	13.12.43	G
21	Lock 16, Maffles	LH U leaf and LH D leaf destroyed	16.12.43 – 15.3.44	G
22	Lock 6, Blaton	D gate and LH U leaf destroyed	31.3.44 – 19.11.44	G
23	Delcourt bridge, Ladeuze	Pontoon sunk	8.4.44	G
24	Ladeuze	Socol pontoon sunk	12.5.44	G
25	Lock 15, Ladeuze	D gate and LH U leaf destroyed. Masonry badly damaged	30.5.44 – 7.12.44	G
26	Rail bridge, U from lock 3, Blaton	Masonry damaged	30.5.44	G
27	Lock 11, Belceil	D gate destroyed	9.6.44 – 7.12.44	G
28	Lock 11, Belceil	U gate destroyed. Masonry (hollow quoin and sill) badly damaged.	12.6.44 – 7.12.44	G

29	Locks 12 to 15	Destruction of transformer houses for locks 12 & 14 and pumps for locks 13 & 15	15.6.44	G
30	Locks 15, Ladeuze	Destruction of elevating pumps	17.6.44	G
31	Locks 11 & 15	Destruction of transformer houses	17.6.44	G
		C/. ANTOING – POMMEROEUL canal		
32	Verne Aqueduct, Roucourt	Masonry destroyed under the canal bed and canal emptied	13.6.43	
33	Aqueduct de la Fontaine Bouillante, Blaton	Masonry destroyed under the canal bed and canal emptied	19.8.43 – 20.9.43	G
34	Lock 6, Moubray	D gate and LH U leaf destroyed	25.11.43	
35	Lock 10, Péronnes	U gate and RH leaf D gate damaged	13.1.44 – 22.2.44	
36	Lock 13, Péronnes	RH leaf U gate destroyed	24.2.44 – 30.4.44	
37	Lock 7, Maubray	RH leaf U gate destroyed	6.3.44 – 6.5.44	
38	Drainage aqueduct, Roucourt	Destruction of drainage channels of canal	15.6.44	
39	Lock 2(?) Harchies	D metal gate destroyed. Masonry badly damaged	23.7.44	G
		D/. MONS-CONDE Canal		
40	Lock 5, Malmaison	D lifting gate badly damaged	26.8.43	G
41	Lock 3, St Ghislain	U gate destroyed. RH D leaf out of action	12.9.43 – 10.11.43	G & AB
42	Bas Flénu railway bridge, Quaregnon	Bridge destroyed. Engine run into the gap	4.12.43 – 13.12.43	G & PA
43	Lock 5, Malmaison	D gate damaged again	10.12.43 – 18.12.43	G

44	Thulin draw-bridge	Destruction of operating mechanism	3.2.44 – 10.2.44	G
45	Bridge, Quievrain – Mainvault, Pommereul	Destruction of bridge	2.6.44	
46	Debihan-sur-la-Haine dam, Thulin	Destruction of the sluice valves of the dam supplying the canal	11.7.44	G
47	Rivages wooden bridge, St Ghislain	Engine allowed to run into the waterway	13.7.44 – 19.7.44	G
48	Thulin wooden bridge	Destruction of piers and floor of the bridge	13.7.44	G
49	Rivages wooden bridge, St Ghislain	Destruction of piers and floor of the bridge	27.7.44 – 2.8.44	
50	Colliery wooden bridge, Hensies	Engine allowed to run into the waterway	28.5.44 – 10.9.44	G
51	Wooden bridge of Herbières lock, Tartre	Destruction of piers and floor of the bridge	31.8.44	
52	Wooden bridge of Quaregnon	Rail-car allowed to run into canal. Floor of bridge damaged	31.8.44	G & CF25
		E/. "CENTRE" canal		
53	Le Thiriau spillway, la Louviere	Destruction of beams of masonry	18.11.43 – 2.1.44	
54	High tension pylon, Oberg	Sabotage. Pylon felled across canal	17.1.44 – 22.1.44	G
55	Wharf Union Chimique factory, Havre-Ville	Sabotage of tanker Standard 26	15.7.44 – 20.7.44	

Notes On List Of Acts Of Sabotage Against Canals In Western Hainault

These notes below refer to items with the same number in the list.

5. A charge placed against the upstream gate failed to explode.

10. Carried out by Carlos (EGC/GB/RS/1322, App. 'A' item 1)

11. Carried out by Carlos. Item 2; Carlos claims 15 days out of action.

12. Carried out by Carlos. Item 6; Carlos claims 5 months out of action, and says that 25 tons of masonry were destroyed, corresponding very well with the 15 metres of wall reported by Draily. The upstream gates were opened for the attack and the charge was placed in the angle between the left-hand downstream gate and the lock wall (i.e. the wall separating the lock from the river). He further reports an unsuccessful attack on the same lock three days previously.

17. Caused the reach above lock 16 to run dry.

19. Drained the reach between locks 10 and 11.

21. Carried out by Carlos (EGC/GB/RS/1322, App. 'A' item 23)

25. Reach upstream from lock 15 drained.

32. This aqueduct was a three-course brick arch 60 cm thick, with 50 cm of earth and clay above it. The charge used was 20 kg.

See accompanying photographs, two of the actual canal bed and damaged vault (and two of the damage done to the bank of the canal 3 km away at CALLENELLE (M.R. J/0122). This damage at a distance, which occurred in other cases, is probably due to the bank at that point being waterlogged, and collapsing when the supporting pressure of the water in the canal was removed by drainage through the damaged aqueduct (port engineers, e.g. at Antwerp, were much concerned regarding this type of collapse if the Germans had demolished locks at the entrance to the old basins).

33. See two accompanying photographs.

40. See eight accompanying photographs.

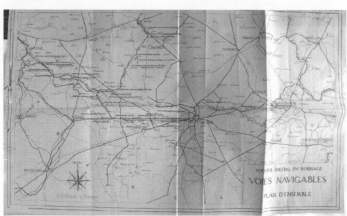

Photograph 3, showing damage to lifting lock gate of the Malmaison lock, Mons-Conde Canal, 26th September, 1943.

Photographs 1 and 2, showing damage caused to aqueduct under the Antoing-Pommeroeul Canal, damaged by lowering a 20 kg. charge into the Canal, 19th September, 1943.

Images accompanying report.[2]

Sabotage Effected By FFI [French Forces Of The Interior] And Agents Under Directives And Instructions Issued By SOE

Efforts in this direction were mainly planned and successfully carried out against communications (Plans Vert, Tortua, Grenouille and Violet) which contributed largely to the liberation of France by the dislocation of transportation and communications, delaying and preventing the movement of enemy troops during D-Day and post D-Day operations.

A number of industrial installations producing armament, MT and AFV, and aircraft material and components for the German war effort were also attacked.

Some of the more important works of this category were sabotaged with the complicity and assistance of the managements under the arrangement known as 'Blackmail' Scheme, whereby immunity from aerial bombardment and subsequent loss of life was guaranteed provided that the precise instructions issued by London for the destruction of key items of machinery, plant or stocks were carried out and that evidence that the required damage had been done was submitted immediately to London HQ.

No sabotage of ports or port installations was carried out; only small 7-metre bridges were attacked by the FFI.

A schedule of all acts of scorching and sabotage to railways, roads, inland waterways, telecommunications etc., exclusive of enemy action of Allied aerial bombardment, is in course of preparation by the respective Ministries concerned. These detailed statements will be appended to this report. [Foot's Appendix G: Industrial Sabotage]

The following industrial installations were visited: -

Gnome & Rhone Aero Engine & Aircraft Works, Le Mans

No acts of sabotage had been carried out or attempted here and therefore no detailed inspection of the plant was made.

Railway Operations – Le Mans District

The District Engineer of the SNCF informed the Mission that, in general, no organised sabotage had been carried out by the FFI.

Power-current failures and interruptions were practically non-existent and the effect never lasted more than three–four hours. Low voltage was occasionally experienced from 1,500 v to 1,100/900 v due to cutting.

The average interruption to traffic due to derailments was from twenty-four to thirty hours.

The Germans prepared demolitions on a bridge 500 yards from the station, but they were surprised by the Americans' arrival and had no time for other demolition preparations.

Isolated sets of sabotage in the Le Mans district included dropping locos into the turntable pit, causing a stoppage for ten days; and the sabotage of one wheel lathe, since repaired.

The scarcity of trains in this district on D-Day was due to machine-gunning and not to bridge destruction: every loco which moved was shot up.

German railway workers were reinforced from February 1944.

Very few German guards were used to protect railways up to 1943 and afterwards no guards were placed at bridges or on lines.

Further details are included in the relative appendix.

Railway Carriage & Wagon Works (Karel and Fouché), Le Mans
This works was attacked 5.5.44. under instructions issued from London HQ based on recommendations by the Technical Section, but the results obtained were unsatisfactory.

There were three small transformers stepping down from 5,000 v to 220 v, only one was damaged and the oil was not ignited. The damaged transformer was replaced and no serious inconvenience was experienced by the management.

The incendiary action recommended against the paint and oil stores was successful but the results were limited to the destruction of the stores and a certain quantity of post office material and equipment used for fitting up railway mail coaches. The fire was not communicated to other parts of the works.

An attempt was made to put the railway turntable out of action but the charge was wrongly sited and placed against one of the heavy cast-iron wheels running on the circumferential track. The explosion only cracked the wheel and did not affect the working of the turntable. The charge should have been applied to the central pivot of the table.

The only other attempt was made against a band saw of no vital importance, to which slight damage was done; this was easily repaired.

The output from this works was not seriously impaired by the attack.

Bronsavia, Paris: ('Blackmail')

This works produces all kinds of A/C equipment, tubing, filters, control apparatus, radio and photographic equipment, gyroscopes, periscopes, optical instruments, bomb sights and fuel-injection apparatus.

The factory was attacked 5.3.44 by a small party with a lorry that was driven inside the works at night and the watchman overpowered.

The transformers, located in the basement, were attacked with HE charges and destroyed as well as the switchboard and the works were thereby shut down.

In addition, a certain number (about fifteen) of precision-grinding machines were destroyed.

One item produced at this works was a fuel-injection and carburettor assembly for aero engines urgently required by the Germans. A small component, consisting of a steel spindle with coned valves and other features accurately ground to very fine limits and weighing only 2 oz, had to be supplied from Germany: the assembly could not be completed without it. Work was frequently held up owing to delays in deliveries of the special component, which arrived in brown paper parcels.

Effective sabotage could be carried out in similar circumstances by preventing the safe arrival of small vital parts supplied from another country or works.

Timkin Ball & Roller Bearing Works, Paris: ('Blackmail')

This important works was attacked 6.4.44 on detailed instructions based on Technical Section's recommendations.

The attack was carried out successfully and resulted in the complete cessation of all production from this works for about three weeks.

At about 10 p.m. a party called at the works and demanded entrance. They parked the lorry inside the courtyard, overcame the watchman and closed the gates. They told the watchman to lead them to the Blanchard face grinders, and when he explained that he knew nothing about this machinery they said it did not matter and then proceeded directly to these machines, fixed their charges to the revolving magnetic clutch feed tables and the column heads of the machines exactly as they had been instructed. Two Blanchard face grinders and two Cincinnati centre-less grinders were destroyed.

Charges were also laid on the air compressors but they omitted to squeeze the time pencils and the charges did not fire.

Charges were placed and fired on a massive cold heading machine, but as they were sited on very robust portions of the frame no damage was done. (Photograph No. 35).

The wrecked grinding machines had been removed and the debris was inspected. There was no possibility of repair, but the management had been able to borrow a Blanchard machine from another works and resume production.

The failures of these compressors, presses, and cold heading machines were of no special importance as this was not included in the task, and the main object of the attack was achieved.

Alcohol Distillery at St Ouen L'Aumone, near Pontoise

Original reports of a successful attack on this distillery claimed the destruction by explosive and incendiary action of 10,000,000 litres of absolute alcohol.

Of the four large storage tanks one was nearly full of molasses. As these tanks were raised on brick pillars about 15 inches high a charge was placed underneath the bottom plate of this tank and one other which did in fact contain 100 per cent alcohol, and it is believed that the conflagration from these two tanks would set fire to the others. The molasses, of course, did not ignite but acted as a fire extinguisher to the burning alcohol from the other tank. The heat from the fire distorted the upper plates of the tanks but the alcohol in them was not ignited.

The two alcohol stills were not attacked though they were specifically mentioned in the instructions.

The total loss of alcohol amounted to only 10,000 litres (2,200 gallons) and not 10,000,000.

The target itself was not of economic or military importance and had been closed down by the Germans for some time past.

Cutting of HT Transmission Lines

The planned policy of constant overturning of HT transmission pylons simultaneously over a wide area was a very important factor in paralysing the enemy's war industries and rail movements.

The lack of power in the Nantes area and elsewhere reflected on the whole military, industrial and economic situation. Without adequate supplies of power, ports cannot be cleared, public utilities, shipyards and factories cannot operate, and unemployment becomes rife with the tendency to develop extreme sentiments. Owing to bombardment of workers' districts men are obliged to live away from the town, and as tramways are stopped for want of power their transportation is delayed.

Photographs Nos 33 and 34 show HT transmission pylons overturned on the 90 KV line from Tivernon to Luisant.

Rouen Area: All power lines into Rouen had been cut and only the local supply from Grand-Quevilly power station was available which was insufficient for requirements, with the result that current for hospital needs was supplied for twenty-four hours per day but the greater part of the town only had power at night. We had been informed previously that Rouen had ample power as the trams were running. We found that so few were in operation that the power situation was not affected.

Dieppedalle Transformer Station near Rouen: This station was bombed by the Allies 30.10.43, causing very little damage, except to the 16,500-v section which was destroyed. On the next day Resistance Groups blew up two three-phase transformers – 20,000 KVA, with twenty-four single pole breakers.

Chaingy Transformer Station: Bombed by the Allies in February and November 1943. Damage done to a large transformer, which was replaced by a spare one obtained from Eguzon. No sabotage by the enemy of French resistance was attempted here. As at Lion d'Or, Distre, and probably other stations, the Germans had placed an electrified wire fence charged with 5,000 v, round the unpatrolled portion of the station. This was connected to an alarm system, both visual and audio, inside the station.

For further details of sabotage activity by the FFI and agents under SOE direction see special appendix.

Summary

1. Apart from port installations, scorching and sabotage does not appear to have been organised on standard lines or by any central organisation. Local commandos had evidently been given directives, leaving the method of action to their own discretion. Furthermore, a variety of demolition charges were used, from aerial bombs, sea mines and torpedo heads to improvised charges enclosed in plywood casings, in addition to a certain number of standard 'Pioneer' demolition stores, e.g. the 3-kg charge.

Demolition charges are usually far in excess of the weight of explosive sufficient for the job. This is partly due to abundance of stores available which they are unable to remove, e.g. 3 tons of French dynamite to blow up a civilian air-raid shelter and 3- and 2-ton charges of dynamite to destroy a small bridge.

2. Since local commandos have other preoccupations just before evacuating a place, the sabotage or demolition of important objectives has often been left until the last minute and carried out in a haphazard manner. Counter-scorching operations must therefore be prosecuted with greater determination by local groups.

3. When it has been decided to defend an objective against sabotage, early contact must be made with the personnel inside the target whose interest it is to protect it and their livelihood. They should endeavour to ascertain the intentions of the enemy and advise local Resistance groups accordingly.

4. In order to be prepared for any eventuality simulated demolition charges of low power designed to make a loud noise with little effect, or HE charges to cause apparent damage to unimportant parts of the plant should be prepared in advance and placed for firing at a moment's notice by inside personnel. Time is thereby given to outside elements to

reach the objective before the enemy can carry out his own demolition.

5. Access to vital parts should be booby-trapped. Heavy oil fires should be started near vulnerable points, producing volumes of black smoke to confuse and prevent the enemy from placing and firing his charges.

6. Full use should be made of the German Road Signs, Warnings and Notice Boards. These should conform strictly to German design and letter characters. In addition to their use for de-routing traffic, they should be prepared in advance and posted as soon as the simulated charges have been blown. This may discourage enemy demolition squads from entering and examining a job already done, especially when they are anxious to escape.

7. As a last resort – when enemy demolition charges have been laid in advance – endeavour to find charges, leads and firing points and make arrangements to cut or sterilise them or replace them by dummy charges.

8. Many German demolition squads have arrived at the last moment with lorry loads of bombs, torpedoes and other explosive stores, which they sometime fire on the lorry after placing it close to the objective. Prepare mines, obstructions or ambushes on approaches to the target to prevent charges reaching their destination.

9. If the target is in an isolated locality ascertain position of local explosive dump and lorry park and attack vehicles there or leaving there.

10. As a last resort, if the enemy persists in efforts to sabotage, local resistance groups should fight it out around the target, where retreating Germans have shown little desire to remain if opposition is shown. The approach of a single plane has caused a demolition squad to abandon their work and evacuate hastily.

11. Do not disdain attempts by management to bribe local German Commander to refrain from or modify demolitions and sabotage. If the local Commander is a temporary officer and a technical or business man in private life, appeal to his professional pride and conscience to refrain from wanton destruction.

12. After evacuation by the enemy continue to protect target until there is no possible chance of further attack. They have returned five days afterwards with devastating results.

Conclusion

1. We have not made enough use of managements and owners of installations who, whilst unable to do physical acts of sabotage, can be contacted and from whom technical advice can be obtained which we, in turn, can pass on to saboteurs.

There should always be a gap between management and staff in matters of this nature.

2. More trouble should be taken – even in the field – to obtain from local sources and managements the latest intelligence as to bottlenecks in production. A vital component may have to be supplied from Germany: concentrate on delaying and preventing the arrival of this article by mistakes in ordering and physical interference in transit.

3. Let SOE or RAF persuade managements to disperse and divide factories, by simulated raids and acts of sabotage, then get managements to exploit dispersal as unavoidable cause of delays in deliveries from one factory to another. Our experience establishes the fact that nationals of the occupied country know far more of local conditions and people than German controllers or ourselves ever learned and, provided that we furnish a reason, they will find means to reduce output required by the enemy.

4. Make the utmost use of our 'Blackmail' methods where patriotic incentive is insufficient. Even if the Germans suspect internal sabotage, they must expand manpower to stop or keep it under control.

5. No target of an industrial or commercial nature should ever be attacked until the agents or operators have been briefed personally by officers of the Technical Section. Too many plants have been entered successfully and then all effort wasted on parts of no importance, whereas with proper briefing the same or less effort would have brought the target to a standstill. The work of all departments is thus wasted and the life of the agent risked for no possible result (vide report of attack on Karel & Fouche, Le Mans, and Alcohol Distillery at St. Ouen L'Aumone).

6. When planning long-term effect choose targets which affect as many industrial and transportation targets as possible, and which give opportunities for successful escape and repetitions of the operations, e.g. electric pylon cutting and overturning.

7. When briefing agents locally let them more into the picture by giving reasons why they are asked to attack the particular objective, and emphasise the result of failure or inaction, i.e. aerial bombardment and long-term destruction of power plant as against short-term and easily repairable pylon cutting.

8. Greater efforts should be made to synchronise our attacks. Many simultaneous acts of the same nature have cumulative effects and take a long time to repair; disruption is caused over a wider area and so prevents compensation and cannibalisation repairs from an undamaged area.

9. Everywhere we found that it is a fallacy to think that the man on the spot knows best. Local leaders often complained of lack or direction from London. In enemy-occupied areas the local population live in a vacuum and know little of what is happening in the next town; to leave the choice of objective to the local leader or agent is dangerous. He may feel there is nothing in his area worth attacking if he is not directed to do so by us. If he makes a decision he is apt to be uncertain that he has acted rightly or usefully.

10. It is also a fallacy to think that the local man, even when he knows the objective, always knows the best way to attack the vulnerable point, or even which is the most vulnerable point. He and his colleagues usually have only a limited knowledge of the process on a large plant, and unless helped by the management must depend on us for guidance.[3]

*

It has been said that nothing is so tedious and so illuminating as a bare list of acts of sabotage, though Selborne sent a long one to the chiefs of staff in January 1944, in support of a declaration of faith in SOE. The list below may nevertheless retain a certain interest; it is compiled from notes made by Brooks when he was sent round France in the winter of 1944/5 to investigate all the claims of industrial sabotage inflicted by F section, and some of the outstanding RF operations of the same kind. A total of about 3,000 lbs (1,360 kg) of explosive – plastic in almost every case – was required to inflict this substantial quantity of damage.

APPENDIX G:
Industrial Sabotage

Place	Firm	Product	Date	Results	Notes
Decazeville		Coal	24-Aug-43	10 days' stop	Lift gear broken
			01-Jan-44	1 day's stop	Winch damaged
			03-Jan-44	2 days' reduced production	Electricity cut off
			25-Jan-44	2 days' stop	Pit exit shaft blocked
			28-Feb-44	4 days' stop	Transformer destroyed
			19-Mar-44	Output cut to 20 per cent for eight weeks	Extraction gear damaged
			30-May-44	3 months' stop of cableway	Three of eight charges did not explode
			07-Jun-44	Electricity cut for two weeks	Skipp destroyed
			11-Jun-44	2 weeks' stop	Winch gear destroyed.
			13-Jun-44	6 weeks' stop on surface workings	Management thereafter agreed to suspend production till liberated
Sochaux-Montbéliard	Peugeot	Tanks	05-Nov-43	3 months' stop	First 'blackmail' operation
			10-Feb-44	Several months' stop	Replacement machine tools destroyed on arrival from Germany
Sochaux-Montbéliard	Peugeot	Aircraft parts	About 15 Jan 44	3 weeks' stop	
			10-Feb-44	5 weeks' stop	Replacement machine tools destroyed on arrival from Germany

Location	Company	Product	Date	Effect	Notes
Eguzon, Indre			15-Mar-44	Output cut to 40 per cent	Replacement machine tools destroyed on arrival from Germany
Chaigny-Orleans-Figeac	Ratier	Electricity	10-Oct-42	Short stop	
		Electricity	25-Apr-43	Trivial stop	
Courbevoie	Bronzavia	Aircraft parts	Jan-44	Stop till liberation	
		Variable pitch propellors	04-Apr-44	3 weeks stop, production never again over 90 per cent	3 Germans killed
Boulogne-sur-Seine	Air Liquide	Compressed air, etc.	11-Nov-43	Slight delay	Charges faultily laid
			19-Mar-44	2 weeks' stop, permanent stop for liquid oxygen; 25 per cent cut for the rest	Production engineer's advice not taken
Asnières	Timken	Ball bearings	06-Apr-44	2 weeks' stop; never again over 28 per cent	Workmen encouraged to go slow
Aubervilliers, Seine	Malicet & Blin	Ball bearings	19-May-44	Production reduced to 20 per cent for some weeks	
Boulogne-sur-Seine	Renault	Tanks	28-Apr-44	Production reduced to 20 per cent for three months; eight tanks damaged; armoured car stolen	
Ivry-sur-Seine	C.A.M.	Ball bearings	17-May-44	Production reduced to 80 per cent	Poor choice of targets
Levallois-Perret, Seine	Arsénal national	Light artillery	19-Feb-44	4 weeks' stop; never back in full production	
Sevran, S-et-O	Westinghouse	Brakes	02-Jul-44	Production reduced to 20 per cent for six weeks	Successful counter-scorch
Beaumont-sur-Oise, S-et-O	Poilet et Chausson	Cement	09-May-44	6 weeks' stop	Factory already out of action – no coal

Location	Company	Product	Date	Result	Notes
Montataire, Creil, Oise	Brissoneaux & Lotz	Rolling stock	14-Jul-44	Production reduced to 70 per cent for 12 weeks	Three out of four compressors damaged
			18-Jan-44	1 week's stop	Transformers damaged
			01-May-44	Production reduced to 70 per cent for eight weeks	Two compressors damaged
Choisy-an-bac	Engelbert	Tyres	23-Jul-44	8 weeks' stop	Large fire; and power house damaged
Dieppedalle, Rouen		Electricity	31-Oct-44	Over six months' stop	
Mantes-Gassicourt	Cellophane	Cellophane	Dec-44	Complete stop of fibrane burnt	
Déville-lès-Rouen, Seine inf	Sté fçse. des Metaux	Machine tools	10-Oct-44	2 weeks' stop; production reduced by half for over six months	
Mantes, S-et-O	C.I.M.T.	Rolling stock	25-Sep-44	Compressor destroyed; two days' stop	Second 2lb charge on second compressor did not explode
			02-Nov-44	10 days' stop	
Fives-Lilles, Nord	Ateliers de Fives-Lille	Locomotives	27-Jun-44	Production reduced to 20 per cent for four days	
			03-Oct-44	2 days' stop	Wrong cranes attacked
Roubaix, Nord	Air Liquide	Compressed air	15-Jun-44	4 weeks' stop	
			17-Jul-44	13 weeks' stop	
Liévin, Pas de Calais	Sté fçse. des Essences	Petrol	04-Jul-44	Stop till after liberation	Attack within two days of shift of product to Germans
Clermont-Ferrand	Chartoir	Aero engine parts	31-Dec-43	1 week's stop	
Lille	Jean Crepelle	Compressed air	18-Jul-44	Stop	
Willems, Nord	Imperator	Oil refinery	07-Nov-43	All stocks burnt	Fire

Location	Company	Target	Date	Effect	Remarks
Douai-Corbehem, Nord	Paix	Oil refinery	20-Aug-44	Most of factory burnt out	Attackers unknown; their stores probably British
Clermont-Ferrand	Michelin	Tyres	03-Jun-43	Over 300 tons of tyres burnt	
			26-Nov-43	Some vehicles taken; a few tyres burnt	Charges did not explode' had they done so, stop would have been total
			05-Dec-43	Nil	
Blois	Bronzavia	Wireless equipment	21-May-44	2 weeks' stop; then slow running till liberation	Destroyed transformer; replaced from chocolate factory
Montluçon	S.A.G.E.M.	Anti-tank guns and sound detectors	21-Jan-44	Production reduced	
			29-Feb-44	Sixtectors destroyed	Leader trained himself from parachuted booklet
Montluçon	Dunlop	Tyres	29-Apr-44	2 weeks' stop	Production had just restarted after air raid in September 1943
			28-Jun-44	Water pump destroyed; no delay	
			25-Jul-44	Stop in lorry tyre shop till liberation	
Prémery, Nièvre	Lambiotte	Acetone etc.	07-Oct-43	Small fire	Transformer destroyed
			29-Apr-44	6 weeks' stop; production reduced till liberation	
			03-May-44	100,000 litres acetone etc. burnt	

Fourchambault, Nièvre	S.N.A.A.C.	Aircraft	20-Sep-43	Output cut to 20 per cent for eight weeks	Most charges discovered and removed
Teillet-Argenty, near Montluçon	C.E.L.C.	Electricity	20-Oct-43	Slight	
			16-Dec-43	1 week's stop; 22 tons oil lost; then output cut to 20 per cent for eight weeks and to 40 per cent till after liberation	
Tulle-Correze	Arsénal national	Guns?	07-Jan-44	Almost total stop	Auxilliary power supply destroyed; main grid constantly interrupted thereafter
Tulle-Virevialle	Arsénal national	Electricity	14-Dec-43	8 tons oil lost; one week's stop	
		Hydro-electricity	23-Feb-44	6 weeks' stop	
Limoges-St Marc		Hydro-electricity	24-Jun-44	6 weeks' stop; then output cut by two-thirds for two weeks and by one third for one week more	
Bussy, The. Vienne		Hydro-electricity	Jul-43	3 weeks' stop	
Bussy, The. Vienne		Hydro-electricity	22-May-44	12 weeks' stop; output then cut by two-thirds	Unnecessarily violent attack
Limoges-Des-Cassaux		Electricity	28-May-43	Output cut by two-thirds for 15 months	Go-slow on repairs
Eguzon, Indre		Electricity	31-Dec-43	80 tons oil lost; 12 weeks' stop	One man set two small charges
Brive-la-Galliarde, Corrèze	Phillips	Wireless valves	21-Oct-43	4 weeks' reduced output	Vacuum pump and experimental equipment destroyed
			26-Mar-44	Output almost stopped till liberation	Blast damage severe

					Damage attributed to defective coal
Ancizes, Puy-de-Dome	Aubert & Duval	Steel	16-May-43	12 weeks' stop	
			13-Nov-43	4 weeks' reduced output	
			08-Feb-44	Water reservoir badly damaged	
Ussel, Corrèze	Montupet	Aluminium cylinder heads	19-Apr-44	2 days' stop	Co-operative management
			02-May-44	Stop till after liberation	Workers also engaged in passive sabotage
			20-Jun-42	2 days' stop	
			11-Dec-42	8 months' stop	
			25-Mar-44	4 weeks' stop, then output cut by 85 per cent till liberation	
Bar, Corrèze		Hydro-electricity	26-May-44	4 months' stop	40 German soldiers on guard, since Tulle arsenal was supplied from here. Conduit into Tulle attacked and destroyed
Carmaux, Tarn	Cie Gle Industrielle	Textiles	03-Apr-44	1 day's stop; slight fall in output	Transformer spares available
Tarascon-sur-Ariège	Forges d'Alais & Camargue	Aluminium	06-May-44	Slight delay	Though factory power plant was destroyed, grid provided future power supply
Bordères-Louron, Htes. Pyr, Gripp, Htes. Pyr	Sté. Des Produits Azotés Bordères	Chemicals	08-Feb-44	6 weeks' stop	
			30-Apr-44	6 weeks' stop	
Montbartier, Tarn & Garonne	Sté. Hydro-electr. De la Moyenne Garonne	Hydro-electricity Copper	20-Mar-44	4 weeks' stop, output cut by 50 per cent till liberation	

Location	Company	Target	Date	Effect	Notes
Sté. Lary, H-Pyr		Electricity	14-Apr-44	Output cut by 50 per cent till liberation	
Sarrancolin, H-Pyr	Alais, Froges & Camargue	Aluminium	13-Mar-44	2½ weeks' stop on local power supply	Main output not affected; corundum by-product stopped for period shown
			09-Apr-44	2 months' stop on same	Main output not affected; corundum by-product stopped for period shown
Lavelanet, Ariège		Electricity	27-Mar-44	24 tons oil burnt; 7 transformers destroyed; output greatly reduced	
Laruns, B-Pyr		Electricity	03-Aug-44	7 weeks' stop	
Lannemazan	S.E.E.A.E. d'Ugine E.E.S-O.	Aluminium	30-May-44	5 months' stop	
Mauzac, Dordogne		Electricity	12-Feb-44	4 months' stop	6 lb explosive failed; engineer damaged equipment involved with hammer and chisel
Tarbes, H-Pyr	Hispano-Suiza	Aero engines	29-Mar-44	2 transformers destroyed	Grid maintained output of seven engines a day, practically unaffected
			13-Apr-44	5 months' stop	Cylinder head casting moulds destroyed
Tarbes, H-Pyr	Arsenal national	Guns	30-Aug-43	Main switchboard destroyed; one day's stop	
			25-May-44	4 months' stop on all 150 mm and 205 mm guns	
Fontpedrouse, Pyr-Or	SNCF	Hydro-electricity	31-Mar-44	3 weeks' stop	
St Georges, T-et-G	SNCF	Hydro-electricity	23-Sep-43	1 day's stop; output cut to 50 per cent for eight weeks	

Location	Company	Product	Date	Effect	Notes
Gesse, Aude	SNCF	Hydro-electricity	23-Sep-43	10 days' stop; then output cut to 15 per cent for four weeks	
Escouloubres, Aude	SNCF	Hydro-electricity	23-Sep-43	4 weeks' stop	
Usson, Ariège		Hydro-electricity	23-Jul-44	8 weeks' stop	
Carcanières Ariège		Hydro-electricity	23-Jul-44	1 day's stop	
Pau	Sté fçse. D'Optique et de Mécanique	Optical Instruments	12-Apr-44	8 weeks' stop; then output cut to 50 per cent	Machine tools attacked
			05-May-44	Took two weeks to repair	Power plant attacked, reinsurance
Lannemazan	Sté. des Produits Azotes	Various metals and chemicals	20-Jul-43	A little oil lost	Transformer attacked but rapidly repaired
			08-Jan-44	One engineer injured	Engineer removed charges before they exploded
			16-Feb-44	New compressor destroyed	It had arrived that afternoon
			26-Feb-44	2 days' stop on manganese production	
			26-May-44	Compressor destroyed; no more hydrogen produced until after liberation	
Bourges	S.C.A.C.	Transport aircraft	07-Aug-44	19 aircraft destroyed; stop on further production	
Bagnères de Bigorre	Lorraine Deitrich	Self-propelled gun carriers	13-May-44	6 months' stop; 48 machine tools etc. damaged or destroyed	

Lyons	Bronzavia	Aircraft engine parts	27-Jan-44	15 machine tools and 42 engines attacked; all but three engines destroyed or badly damaged; 4 weeks' stop then cut to 40 per cent till September	Police informed half-horly by telephone that all was well
Lyon-Villeurbanne	Le Roulement	Ball bearings	11-Nov-43	2 weeks' stop	Transformer damaged
			23-Apr-44	2 weeks' stop; output then cut to 30 per cent	Sevon machine tools attacked; police removed two charges
Gardanne, B-d-R	Forge d'Alais and Camargue	Aluminium	13-Jun-42	Output cut for several months	One-man job
			30-Apr-43	Output cut for several months	One-man job
			05-Mar-44	Output cut to 40 per cent for over a year	15 men at work
Grenoble	Brun	Alcohol	07-Jul-43	Plant destroyed	One attacker killed by a guard
Grenoble	F.I.T.	Rubber	13-Jul-44	3,000 tyres burnt; 4 months' stop	
Salindres, Gard	Forges d'Alais & Camargue	Aluminium?	08-Jun-44	Slight cut in output	Three out of four boiler pump feeds destroyed
L'Estaque, B-d-R	Kuhlmann	Chemicals	16-Apr-44	300 tons oil burnt; output unaffected	
St Marcel, B-d-R	Coder	Rolling stock	20-Jun-44	Three compressors destroyed; output unaffected	
			14-Jul-44	Three compressors destroyed; one week's stop; output cut to 90 per cent	Two spare compressors overlooked
Béziers, Hérault	Fouga	Locomotives	21-Apr-44	One compressor destroyed; output cut to 90 per cent	Charge on second compressor failed

Location	Company	Product	Date	four months	
Notre-dame de Briançon, Htes. Alpes	S.E.E.A.E.	Hydro-electricity	08-May-43	Conduit cut; some fall in output	
L'Eau Rousse,	S.E.E.A.E	Hydro-electricity	10-Jul-43	1 month's stop	
			12-Aug-43	Conduit cut; some fall in output	
			29-Nov-43	2 months' stop	Rebuilt by spring
			? 23 Jan 44	Spare transformer destroyed	Both alternators heavily damaged
			25-Jan-44	4 months' stop; output then much reduced	
Ugine	S.E.E.A.E	Hydro-electricity	13-Dec-43	2 weeks' stop	
			28/12/1943 onwards	Conduit under constant attack	Firm fell back on two auxilliary pumps
			25-Mar-44	Both auxilliary pump motors destroyed; one week's stop	Much slight sabotage followed
			05-May-44	Mechanical coal supply heavily damaged; large cut in output	
			06-May-44	Cables cut; two days' stop	
Notre-dame de Briançon	Sté. Des Electrodes de la Savoie	Electrodes	24-Oct-43	2½ months' stop	
			25-Jan-44	3 months' stop	
Annecy, The. Savoie	S.R.O.	Ball bearings	13-Nov-43	3 days' stop; two weeks' partial output	
			25-Nov-44	15 machine tools attacked; output slowly raised to 40 per cent	Two charges failed

St Etienne	Nadella	Ball bearings	30-Apr-44	Eight machines destroyed	70 more had unitiated charges
Lyon-Vénisseux	S.I.G.M.A.	Aircraft engine parts	27-Nov-43	1 week's stop; output partial only for three weeks more	Four transformers and a compressor damaged; choice of target bad. Plant engineer said later 'far more damaged could have been done by hitting each crankshaft in stock with a haammer and aslo by attacking four rectifiers which were impossible to replace.'
Lyon-St Fonds	Paris-Rhone	Electrical equipment	20-Jan-44	1 week's stop; output thereafter 60–70 per cent	
Lyon-Vénisseux	S.O.U.M.A.	Rolling stock, armour etc.	26-Feb-44	1 week's stop; output up to 70 per cent in a week more, except in heavy machining which was up to 30 per cent after two months	Plant was armouring a German train. Over 30 unexploded charges.
Belfort	Alsthom	Shell cases	01-Oct-43	Two pumps destroyed; stop in one shop for three months	Go-slow over repairs
Belfort	Lorraine	Half-track fighting vehicles	16-Jul-44	Five half-tracks destroyed. Wehrmacht had taken delivery that day	
Le Creusot?	Cie Bourguignonne de Transport d'Energie	Electricity	08-Sep-43	Slight fall in output	Wrong sub-station attacked

Source: Foot, M. R. D, *SOE in France: an Account of the Work of the British Special Operations Executive in France, 1940-1944* (London: Frank Cass, 2004), pp. 453–65

Conclusion

After D-Day, the RAF Film Unit used Brickendonbury for some scenes in a documentary film entitled *School for Danger*. It featured Harry Rée and Jacqueline Nearne playing the part of SOE agents in France. One scene showed a 'student' placing a charge on an electrical transformer and then running for cover behind a blast wall. Another showed an instructor using a model of a steam railway engine to show 'students' the best places to plant explosives. The film was released in 1946 as *Now It Can Be Told* and clips from it were featured in Rée's interview in the grounds for a 1980s documentary, *The Secret War*.

When the war finished in June 1945, Brickendonbury reverted to a more peaceful role. The mansion was taken over by the Highways Department of Hertfordshire County Council and as offices for the local branches of the National Agricultural Advisory Service and the War Agricultural Executive. The grounds were largely left unmanaged and much of the interior of the mansion was painted beige, like so many government buildings at the time.

In 1970 it was one of the locations chosen for the filming of London Weekend Television's second series of *Catweazle*, a children's programme featuring an eleventh-century wizard appearing in the

1970s and mistaking twentieth-century technology as powerful magic.

In 1971 the mansion, various other buildings and the 40-acre estate were purchased by the Malaysian Rubber Producers' Research Association and a reminder of the estate's wartime activities was found during restoration work in 1973, when unexploded hand grenades and live mortar shells were discovered while the moat was being drained. A bomb disposal unit had to be called in to deal with it. The pool had a large crack in it, thought to have been caused by a carelessly lobbed hand grenade.

In 1974 it became known as the Tun Abdul Razak Research Centre, after Malaysia's second Prime Minister. The grounds were revived and Brickendonbury has become home to a research laboratory and promotion centre. The mansion, both inside and out, has been restored to provide elegant working accommodation, and the grounds are well cared for. The purpose-built laboratories, housing the practical work of the Research Centre, are in part concealed behind the facade of the Pearson's model farm, which still retains the family motto.

It is of interest that some of the staff in the twenty-first century refer to the house as 'Brickers', in the same way as British ex-pats called Peking 'Peekers' and Hong Kong 'Honkers'. Few realise that the site used to house Brica's tribe.[1]

The contribution made by Brickendonbury and its graduates to the outcome of the Second World War has received little coverage in military histories. In Rheam's recommendation for an Order of the British Empire medal (OBE), Gubbins stated that

> The success achieved by S.T.S. 17 has been directly due to the efforts of Lt. Col. Rheam. At the time when he joined S.O.E., industrial sabotage was in its rudimentary stages, and it is by his great knowledge of engineering, coupled with his tireless energy, devotion to duty and his ability to inspire those working under him, that the present methods both of training and operation have been brought to their present high standard.
>
> In addition to his contribution to the development of industrial sabotage in general, great praise is due to him for his work in

connection with special operations and 'Coup de Main' parties. The success achieved in this sphere is undoubtedly very largely due to the painstaking efforts of Lt. Col. Rheam, first in evolving suitable methods of attack, and also in the thoroughness of the training given to the parties in which no detail was too small to warrant his personal attention.[2]

Aware of the potential of 'unattributable' sabotage, the SOE realised that similar training establishments in other parts of the British Empire could increase the numbers of potential saboteurs overseas. They liaised with William Stephenson, codenamed Intrepid, a Canadian entrepreneur who ran the British Security Coordination in New York. It was with Stephenson's assistance that the government in Canada agreed to Project J, an SOE training school close to the US border at Whitby, on the banks of Lake Ontario. Its aim was to train Canadians and Americans in paramilitary warfare. Opened on 6 December 1941, the Royal Canadian Mounted Police called it S25-1-1 and SOE called it STS 103, but it became better known as Camp X. It was staffed by SOE-trained officers and included similar courses to those being taught in England and Scotland. Its demolitions instructor was twenty-five-year-old Major Frederick Milner. Lynn Hodson, the Camp X historian, reported that 'the ever popular Major Milner treated many top officials from the SOE, the Federal Bureau of Investigation and the British Security Coordination to a fascinating exhibition of "fireworks"'.[3]

The camp's cover was an explosives testing ground and, according to David Stafford, who researched Camp X, Milner had a constant demand for explosives and was helped by Canadian Industries Limited, from whom he purchased the ordnance equipment on which his students practiced their industrial sabotage.[4]

The American intelligence service, developed by William Donovan the Coordinator of Information, became known in 1942 as the OSS, the Office of Strategic Services. While in Britain on a fact-finding mission about the country's determination to fight Nazism, Donovan was given full access to the SOE's training schools. Although undocumented, it seems very likely he was shown around Brickendonbury. Needing to train American agents to undertake OSS-inspired clandestine warfare, he established similar training schools to the SOE in the United States.

A training school in the Catoctin Mountain Park in Maryland opened in early 1942. Known as Area B, here Gleason taught industrial sabotage to OSS recruits for Special Operations.[5] One of Gleason's fellow instructors on the sabotage course was Captain Charles Parkin. After the war, Roosevelt called the camp Shang Ri La and Eisenhower renamed it Camp David.[6]

Following the Allies' success in taking control of North Africa, other Brickendonbury graduates were sent to Algiers where a training school was set up outside 'Massingham', SOE's codename for its base in Algiers. Rheam's demolition training was one of the subjects on its curriculum.[7] SOE also had training schools in Olokomeji, 30 miles from Ibadan in Nigeria, where Sergeant Quigley from the Royal Engineers was the demolitions instructor. He was assisted by Corporal C. Davis, Corporal C. Morgan and Sergeant Major Ali Zebo. There was another at the Nanwa Gold Mines in the Ashanti area, which could accommodate up to forty students; Sergeant Quigley was their demolitions instructor. As well as demolitions, students had drill, unarmed combat, weapons training, scouting, map reading, observation and reports, first aid, patrolling, guerilla warfare, fieldcraft and schemes. Both schools had a drill square, games field, assault course, small arms ranges, grenade range, demolition area, magazine, lecture room, display room and a 50-metre model railway. A third school was to be located in Sierra Leone but it is unknown if it was completed and it is likely that there was another in the Durban area of South Africa for training agents for missions in Mauritius and Madagascar.

The SOE also set up similar training schools in Tanjong Balai in Singapore (STS 101), Ramat David, in Haifa, Palestine (STS 102), Italy, and following the liberation of France in chateaux south-west of Paris in late 1944. Very likely their demolitions instructors had been to Brickendonbury and received their training from Rheam.[8]

The impact of both direct and indirect sabotage on the Germans' war effort cannot be accurately measured but, according to Cyril

Cunningham, it must have been colossal. 'The resistance ultimately made it impossible for the Germans to move about outside the main centres of population except in armoured convoys. Life for the ordinary German soldier in any occupied town was made unsafe and miserable.'[9] The constant sabotage, both large- and small-scale operations, must have driven the Germans to distraction. Diverting men to anti-sabotage duties also reduced the numbers available for front-line duties.

Brickendonbury-trained instructors ensured the sabotage of the Norwegian, Danish, Dutch and Belgian railway and shipping in the days before and on D-Day, which was reported by Foot to have delayed German reinforcements reaching Normandy by at least a week. The French resistance delayed some Panzer divisions in the South of France for up to two weeks. This allowed the Allies to develop their bridgehead and make their push towards Paris against fewer enemy troops.

The impact that Brickendonbury-inspired sabotage had on the morale of the resistance groups and the general population in other occupied countries must have been highly significant. Hopefully this book will ensure that Brickendonbury's role in the outcome of the Second World War will not be forgotten.

Notes

1 Brickendonbury Manor's History until the Start of the Second World War, September 1939

1 http://www.brickendonbury.co.uk/pages/Our%20Great%20Estate.pdf
2 Email communication with Graham Irwin, 14 April 2012.
3 'Story of Brickendonbury', in *Hertfordshire Countryside*, September 1988, Vol. 3, pt 353, pp. 30–1.

2 Brickendonbury and the Secret Intelligence Service, September 1939– August 1940

1 Foot, M. R. D., *S.O.E: An Outline History of the Special Operations Executive 1940–46*, Pimlico, 1999, pp. 4–5.
2 Quoted in Turner, D., *SOE's Secret Weapons Centre: STATION 12*, The History Press, 2006, p. 14.
3 Philby, K., *My Silent War*, Macgibbon and Kee, 1968, p. 7.
4 https://www.sis.gov.uk/our-history/buildings.html
5 Philby, op. cit. p. 7.
6 TNA HQ 64, MI R, Functions and Organisation.
7 Hill, G., *Reminiscences of Four Years with the N.K.V.D.*, Private publication, Hoover Institution Archives, 1968, p. 2.
8 Turner, op. cit. pp. 16–17.
9 Hill, op. cit. p. 2.
10 Philby, op. cit. p. 8.
11 Deacon, R., *A History of the British Secret Service*, Muller, London, 1969, p. 302.
12 Philby, op. cit.
13 Philby, op. cit.
14 Philby, op. cit. p. 9.

15 Philby, op. cit. p. 6.

16 Philby, op. cit. pp. 10–11.

17 Mackenzie, W., 2002, 'The Secret History of Special Operations Executive 1940–1945', St Ermin's Press, Special Forces Club website.

18 Philby, op. cit. p. 11.

19 West. N., *MI5: British Security Service Operations, 1909–1945*, Harper Collins, 1983, p. 290.

20 Philby, op. cit. p. 15.

21 Marriott, E., *Claude Péri and Madeleine Bayard: A True Story of War, Espionage and Passion*, Picador, 2005.

22 Quoted in Turner, D., *SOE's Secret Weapons Centre: STATION 12*, The History Press, 2006, p. 8.

3 Brickendonbury and the Special Operations Executive, August 1940– June 1945

1 Ryder, S., *Child of My Love*, Harvill Press.

2 Heath, C., 'Wartime Secret Agents Learned Their Sabotage Tricks at Brickendonbury', in *Herts and Essex Observer*, 16 March 1978 p. 41.

3 Macrae, S., 1971, Winston Churchill's Toyshop, Roundwood Press, p. 8.

4 http://www.bbc.co.uk/ww2peopleswar/stories/34/a5961134.shtml

5 http://www.bbc.co.uk/ww2peopleswar/stories/34/a5961134.shtml

6 Macrae, op. cit. p. 9.

7 http://www.bbc.co.uk/ww2peopleswar/stories/34/a5961134.shtml

8 Macrae, op. cit. p. 9.

9 Author's email communication with Michael Simmonds, 27 March 2012.

10 http://www.bbc.co.uk/ww2peopleswar/stories/34/a5961134.shtml

11 Turner, D., op. cit. pp. 144–5.

12 Macrae, op. cit. p. 11.

13 Macrae, op. cit. p. 20.

14 Macrae, op. cit. p. 94.

15 TNA HS 8/371

16 Macrae, op. cit.

17 Bailey, R., *Forgotten Voices of the Secret War: An Inside History of Special Operations Executive*, Imperial War Museum, 2009.

18 http://www.bbc.co.uk/ww2peopleswar/stories/51/a5961251.shtml

19 Philby, op. cit. p. 8.

20 http://www.bbc.co.uk/ww2peopleswar/stories/15/a5961251.shtm

21 http://en.wikipedia.org/wiki/MD1

22 Macrae, op. cit. p. 56.

23 Macrae, op. cit. p. 155.

24 http://en.wikipedia.org/wiki/PIAT

25 TNA HS 9/321.8.

26 TNA HS9/160/5.

27 http://www.realmilitaryflix.com/public/253.cfm

28 Ryder, op. cit.

29 Binney, M., *Secret War Heroes*, Hodder and Stoughton, 2005.

30 Heath, C. 'Wartime Secret Agents Learned Their Sabotage Tricks at

Brickendonbury', in *Herts and Essex Observer*, 16 March 1978 p. 41.

31 Stafford, D., *Secret Agent: The True Story of the Special Operations Executive*, BBC, 2000, pp. 64–5.

32 Ibid. p. 65.

33 Macrae, op. cit. p. 88, 155–6.

34 TNA HS 9/1250/7.

35 Ibid.

36 Foot, op. cit.

37 Foot, M. R. D., 'The Special Operations Executive SOE in Hertfordshire 1940-1946, *Herts Past and Present*, Autumn 2006, Vol. 3 pt 8 p. 4.

38 TNA HS 9/1250/7.

39 TNA HS 8/229.

40 Ryder, op. cit. p. 80.

41 TNA HS8/370.

42 Foot, M. R. D., 'The Special Operations Executive SOE in Hertfordshire 1940–1946, *Herts Past and Present*, Autumn 2006 Vol. 3 pt 8 p. 4.

43 Jenkins, R., *A Pacifist at War: The Life of Francis Cammaerts*, Hutchinson, London, 2009, p. 64.

44 Stafford, D., op. cit. p. 37.

45 McDonnell, P. K., *Operatives, Spies and Saboteurs*, Citadel Press, 2004, p. 7.

46 Email communication with author, 13 April 2012.

47 Email communication with Tom Colville, 12 April 2012.

48 TNA HS 7/53.

49 Ibid.

50 Ibid.

51 Rigden, D., *How to Be a Spy: The World War II SOE Training Manual*, The National Archives, 2004, pp. 8–9.

52 http://www.bbc.co.uk/history/worldwars/wwtwo/the_plotters_01.shtml

53 TNA HS 9/160/5.

4 Early Sabotage Missions by Brickendonbury 'Graduates', 1940–1

1 Philby, op. cit. pp. 4–5.

2 Philby, op. cit. p. 5.

3 Ibid. p. 6.

4 TNA HS 8/371.

5 *The Belfast Telegraph*, 'German U-boats refuelling in Ireland? Surely not', 19 September 2011.

6 Richards, B., *Secret Flotillas: Clandestine sea operations to Brittany, 1940–1944*, Frank Cass, 2003, p. 87.

7 Richards, B., *Secret Flotillas: Clandestine sea operations to Brittany, 1940–1944*, Frank Cass, 2003.

8 Marriott, E., *Claude Péri and Madeleine Bayard: A True Story of War, Espionage and Passion*, Picador, 2005.

9 Ibid.

10 Reardon, M. J., 'Death at the Hands of Friends: Oran', in *Army History*, Winter 2011, p. 16, 18; Edwards, *Seven Sailors*, Collins, London, 1945, pp. 232–3.

11 Atkinson, R., *An Army at Dawn*, Holt Paperbacks, New York, 2002; Reardon, M. J., 'Death at the Hands of Friends: Oran', in *Army History*, Winter 2011, p. 16.
12 Allied Forces Headquarters, General Orders No. 19, 23 November 1942.
13 Sam McBride's article on the Naval and Military museum's website.
14 Foot, SOE in France, p. 91.
15 Email communication with Waldemar Grabowski.

5 Brickendonbury and Operation Anthropoid: The Assassination of Reinhard Heydrich, Prague, Czechoslovakia, 1942

1 Heath, C., 'Wartime Secret Agents Learned Their Sabotage Tricks at Brickendonbury', in *Herts and Essex Observer*, 16 March 1978 p. 41.
2 http://www.holocaustresearchproject.org/nazioccupation/ heydrichkilling.html
3 TNA HS 4/39.
4 Rees, N., *The Secret History of the Czech Connection: The Czechoslovak Government in Exile in London and Buckinghamshire During the Second World War*, Neil Rees 2005.

6 Brickendonbury and the Sabotage of the Heavy Water Plant at Vemork, Rjukan, Norway, 1942–4

1 TNA HS 2/128 'Norwegian Project', 3 November 1940; HS 2/240, Note headed 'Section D', 7 August 1940.
2 Mears, R., *The Real Heroes of Telemark: The True Story of the Secret Mission to Stop Hitler's Atomic Bomb*, Hodder and Stoughton, 2003, p. 38.
3 TNA HS 9/886/2 Rubin Langmo.
4 'First sabotage action during the war,' in *Bergens Tidende*, 3 September 2001, p. 22; HS 2/241 Norwegian expedition 1940; HS 2/242 Results of Norwegian expedition 1940–1946.
5 Archives of the Trades Union Congress, 292C/946/1/22 i, Warwick University.
6 TNA HS 2/185.
7 Njølstad, O., *Professor Tronstads Krig*, Aschehoug, 2012.
8 TNA HS 2/224; http://www.combinedops.com/Lofoten_Islands_Raid.htm
9 Clark, F., *Agents by Moonlight*, Tempus Publishing, 1999, p. 40.
10 Bailey, R., *Forgotten Voices of the Secret War: An Inside History of the Special Operations Executive*, Random House, 2009, p. 137.
11 www.ww2talk.com/forum/special-forces/29127-telemark-sabotage-battle-heavy-water.html
12 Mears, op. cit. pp. 118–9.
13 Ryder, op. cit. p. 83.
14 Quoted in Mears, op. cit. p. 122.
15 Charrot, J., *Memories of a Navigator of 138 Squadron flying on Special Duties for SOE*, unpublished memoirs 1995 Imperial War Museum 29163.
16 Miller, R., *Behind the Lines: The Oral History of Special Operations in World War II*, Secker and Warburg, 2002, p. 110.
17 Miller, R., op. cit. p. 113.
18 *The Times*, Birger Stromsheim's obituary, 20 November 2012.

19 Mears, op. cit. p. 206.
20 TNA HS 2/173; http://www.pbs.org/wgbh/nova/hydro/mess-01.html
21 Ibid.
22 Ibid.
23 Ibid.

7 Brickendonbury and Blackmail Sabotage: Peugeot Automobile Works,
   Sochaux-Montbéliard, France, 1943–4

1 Quoted in Foot, *SOE in France*, p. 15.
2 TNA HS 7/136.
3 TNA HS 9/1240/3.
4 Ibid.
5 TNA HS 9/1240/3, 1 January 1943.
6 BBC *SOE* 1984, Episode 1 – 'Setting Europe Ablaze'.
7 TNA HS 9/1240/3.
8 TNA HAS 9/1240/3; Binney, M., *Secret War Heroes*, Hodder and Stoughton, 2005.
9 TNA HS 9/1240/3.
10 Foot, M. R. D., *SOE in France: an Account of the work of the British Special
   Operations Executive in France, 1940-1944*, Frank Cass, London, 2004, p. 454.
11 http://peugeot.mainspot.net/hist13.shtml; http://www.cancoillotte.net/spip.
   php?article8; http://www.raf.mod.uk/bombercommand/ jul43.html; Binney
   erroneously reported the attack happening on 14 July, Bastille Day.
12 http://www.cancoillotte.net/spip.php?article8
13 TNA HS 9/1240/3.
14 TNA HS 7/122 Major R. A. Bourne-Paterson's 'British Circuits in France
   1941–1944', 1946
15 Buckmaster, M., *They Fought Alone*, W. W. Norton & Co. 1958, p. 153.
16 Buckmaster, op. cit. p. 155.
17 http://www.cancoillotte.net/spip.php?article8; Bonney, op. cit.
18 TNA HS 7/122.
19 TNA HS 9/1240/3.
20 Buckmaster, op. cit. p. 156.
21 TNA HS 9/1240/3.
22 TNA HS 9/1240/3, 4 October 1943.
23 TNA HS 7/122.
24 TNA HS 9/1240/3.
25 TNA HS 9/1240/3; HS 7/122, Annex A, pp. 65–6; http://www.cancoillotte.
   net/spip.php?article8
26 TNA HS 9/1240/3.
27 Rée, H., Imperial War Museum 13064.
28 http://www.cancoillotte.net/spip.php?article8
29 Buckmaster, op. cit. p. 157.
30 TNA HS 9/1240/3.
31 TNA HS 9/1240/3; Foot, op. cit. p. 454.
32 *The Daily Telegraph*, Colonel Maurice Buckmaster's obituary, April 1992.
33 TNA HS 9/1240/3.
34 TNA HS 7/122, Annex A, pp. 65–6.

35 TNA HS 9/1240/3, 2 November 1943.
36 Ibid.
37 TNA SH 9/1240/3.
38 TNA HS 7/122, Annex A, pp. 65–6.
39 http://www.cancoillotte.net/spip.php?article8
40 TNA HS 9/1240/3.
41 www.spartacus.school.net.co.uk/SOEree.htm
42 TNA HS 9/1240/3.
43 Buckmaster, op. cit.
44 TNA HS 7/122, Annex A, pp. 65–6.
45 http://www.cancoillotte.net/spip.php?article8; TNA HS 7/122; Foot, op. cit. p. 454
46 Ibid.
47 Buckmaster, op. cit. pp. 159–160.
48 Foot, op. cit. p. 454.
49 TNA HS 7/122, Annex A, pp. 65–6.
50 TNA HS 9/1240/3.
51 Ibid. 2 May 1945.
52 TNA HS 9/1240/3, dated 14 June 1945.
53 TNA HS 7/136.

8 Learning from Experience: Insight into Industrial Sabotage by Those Involved

1 TNA HS8/370 SOE/HQ 185.
2 TNA HS 8/415 Industrial Sabotage memorandum.
3 TNA HS 7/136.

Conclusion

1 Heath, C., 'Wartime Secret Agents Learned Their Sabotage Tricks at Brickendonbury', in *Herts and Essex Observer*, 16 Mar 1978 p. 41; 'Story of Brickendonbury', in *Hertfordshire Countryside*, Sep 1988 Vol. 3 pt 353 pp. 30–1; Irwin, G., *What a Liberty!: A History of Brickendon and its Environs including Wormley*, CityScape Books, 2004.
2 TNA HS9 1250/7.
3 http://www.camp-x.com/officers1942.htm
4 Stafford, D., *Camp X*, Lester and Orpen Denys, 1986, p. 72.
5 https://www.cia.gov/news-information/featured-story-archive/office-of-strategic-services-training.html
6 Email communication with Frank Gleason, 21 July 2012.
7 Foot, M. R. D., *S.O.E.: An Outline History of the Special Operations Executive 1940–46*, Pimlico, 1999, p. 91.
8 Email communication with Steven Kippax, 19 and 20 July 2012.
9 Cunningham, C., *Beaulieu: the Finishing School for Secret* Agents, Leo Cooper, London, 1998, p. 81.

Bibliography

Andrew, C. and Gordievsky, *KGB: The Inside Story of its Foreign Operations from Lenin to Gorbachev*, Harper Collins (1990).

Atkinson, R., *An Army at Dawn*, New York: Holt Paperbacks (2002).

Bailey, R., *Forgotten Voices of the Secret War: An Inside History of Special Operations Executive*, Random House (2009).

Berglyd, J., *Operation Freshman: The Actions and the Aftermath*. Solna: Leandoer & Ekholm (2007).

Bind, E., *Kompani Linge Binde*, I, Gyldendal Norsk Forlag (1948) pp. 137–49.

Binney, M., *Secret War Heroes*, Hodder and Stoughton (2005).

Boyce, F. and Everett, D., *SOE: The Scientific Secrets*, The History Press (2003).

Burns, J., *Papa Spy: A True Story of Love, Wartime Espionage in Madrid, and the Cambridge Spies*, Bloomsbury (2011).

Cave Brown, A., *C: The Secret Life of Sir Graham Menzies, Spymaster to Winston Churchill*, Macmillan (1987).

Charrot, J., *Memories of a Navigator of 138 Squadron flying on Special Duties for SOE*, unpublished memoirs (1995). Copy in Imperial War Museum.

Christensen, Dag, *Hemmelig agent i Norge*, Oslo: Hjemmets bokforlag (in Norwegian, 1987).

Clark, F., *Agents by Moonlight*, Tempus Publishing (1999).

Cowburn, B., *No Cloak No Dagger*, Jarrolds (1960).

Crawley, A., 'The Limpet Mine & 171–175 Tavistock Street, Bedford', in *Bedford Architectural, Archaeological & Local History Society* Newsletter 89, April 2012, pp. 17–20.

Crowdy, T., *SOE Agent: Churchill's Secret Warriors*, Osprey Publishing (2008).

Cunningham, C., *Beaulieu: the Finishing School for Secret Agents*, London: Leo Cooper (1998).

Dahl, Per F. (1999), *Heavy Water and the Wartime Race for Nuclear Energy*, London: CRC Press (2007).

Davies, P. H. J., *MI6 and the Machinery of Spying*, Frank Cass (2004).

Deacon, R., *A History of the British Secret Service*, London: Muller (1969).

Edwards, K., *Seven Sailors*, London: Collins (1945).

Fitzsimons, P., *Nancy Wake: The Inspiring Story of One of the War's Greatest Heroines*, Harper Collins (2002).

Foot, M. R. D., *S.O.E.: An Outline History of the Special Operations Executive 1940–46*, Pimlico (1999).

Foot, M. R. D., *SOE in France: An Account of the Work of the Special Operations in France 1940–1945*, Routledge (2004).

Foot, M. R. D., 'The Special Operations Executive (SOE) in Hertfordshire 1940-1946, in *Herts Past and Present*, Autumn 2006, Vol. 3 pt 8 pp. 3–7.

Gjems-Onstad, E., *Durham* and *Lark*, Milorg I Trøndelag (1940–1945).

Grytten, K., Thamshavnbanens Venner, Thamshavnbanen. Orkanger (1983).

Heggem, T., Torfinn Bjørnås obituary, in *Adresseavisen*, 22 September 2009, p. 34.

Hetherinton, I., 'The Special Operations Executive in Norway 1940–1945: Policy and Operations in the Strategic and Political Context', Ph.D dissertation at De Montfort University, Leicester (2004).

Hill, G., *Reminiscences of Four Years with the N.K.V.D*, Private publication, Hoover Institution Archives (1968).

Irwin, G., *What a Liberty!: A History of Brickendon and its Environs including Wormley*, CityScape Books (2004).

Jenkins, R., *A Pacifist at War: The Life of Francis Cammaerts*, London: Hutchinson (2009).

Jensen, Erling; Ratvik, Per; Ulstein, Ragnar, ed. (1948) (in Norwegian) 'Hjemmegjorte torpedoer' (in Norwegian) in *Kompani Linge*. I, Oslo: Gyldendal. p. 326.

Jensen, E, Ratvik, P. and Ulstain, R., *Kompani Linge Binde*, I–II, Oslo (1948).

Kamiya, G. and J. Smith, *Shadow Knights: The Secret War Against Hitler*, Simon and Schuster (2010).

Kilde, K. L., *Resistance Male and politician. From XU to Kings Bay*. Gyldendal (1991).

Knightley, P., *The Master Spy: The Story of Kim Philby*, Vantage Books (1990).

Mackenzie, W., *The 'Secret History of Special Operations Executive 1940–1945*, St Ermin's Press (2002).

Macrae, S., *Winston Churchill's Toyshop*, Roundwood Press (1971).

McDonnell, P. K., *Operatives, Spies and Saboteurs*, Citadel Press (2004).

Mears, R., *The Real Heroes of Telemark: The True Story of the Secret Mission to Stop Hitler's Atomic Bomb*, Hodder and Stoughton (2003).

Miller, R., *Behind the Lines, the oral history of Special Operations in World War II*, London: Secker and Warburg (2002).

Olsen, O. R., *Two Eggs on my Plate*, London Allen and Unwin (1952).

Ording, A; Johnson, Gudrun and Garder, Johan. 'Deinboll, Peter Vogelius' (in Norwegian), in *Våre falne 1939–1945*. *1*. Oslo: The State of Norway (1949).

Otway, Lieutenant-Colonel T. B. H., *The Second World War 1939–1945 Army – Airborne Forces*, London: Imperial War Museum (1990).

Philby, K., *My Silent War*, Macgibbon and Kee (1968).

Pujol, J. and N. West, *Operation GARBO: the personal story of the most successful double agent of World War II*, Random House (1985).

Reardon, M. J., 'Death at the Hands of Friends: Oran', in *Army History*, Winter (2011).

Rees, N., *The Secret History of the Czech Connection: The Czechoslovak Government in Exile in London and Buckinghamshire During the Second World War* (2005).

Richards, B., *Secret Flotillas, Vol. 1: Clandestine Sea Opeartions to Brittany, 1940–1944*, Routledge (2004).

Richelson, J. T., *A Century of Spies: Intelligence in the Twentieth Century*, Oxford University Press (1995).

Rigden, D., *How to Be a Spy: The World War II SOE Training Manual*, The National Archives (2001).

Riley, M., *Philby: The Hidden Years*, Janus Publishing (1999).

Rogers, J. D., *The Race to Build the Atomic Bomb*, lecture notes, Minnesota University.

Rosander, L., *Behind Declassified: Secret operations in Sweden Today*, Historical Media (2004).

Ryder, S., *Child of My Love*, Harvill Press (1997).

Seaman, M., *Garbo: The Spy Who Saved D-Day*, National Archives (2000).

Searle, P. and M. McConville, *Philby, the Long Road to Moscow*, Hamilton (1973).

Stafford, D., *Camp X*, Lester and Orpen Denys (1986).

Stafford, D., *Secret Agent: The True Story of the Special Operations Executive*, BBC Worldwide Limited (2000).

Tickell, J., *Odette*, Chapman and Hall (1949).

Turner, D., *SOE's Secret Weapons Centre: STATION 12*, The History Press (2006).

West, N., *MI5: British Security Service Operations, 1909–1945*, Harper Collins (1983).

West, N., *MI6: British Secret Intelligence Service*, Random House (1983).

Documents in the National Archives

CAB 66/7/7 Nils Nordland
HS 2/128 'Norwegian Project', 3 November 1940
HS 2/240, Note headed 'Section D', 7 August 1940
HS 4/39 Special Operations Executive Eastern Europe Czechoslovakia
HS 6/112 Elaine Madden
HS 8/370 SOE/HQ 185 (Brickendonbury)
HS 8/371 SOE Lectures and Statistics, 1942
HS 8/415 (Industrial) Sabotage (memorandum)
HS 9/321/8 Cecil Clarke
HS 9/413/5 Peter Deinboll
HS 9/886/2 Rubin Langmo
HS 9/924/7 Alf Lindberg
HS 9/986/2 Max Manus

HS 9/1109/4 Nils Nordland
HS 9/1250/7 George Rheam
HS 9/1370/8 Einar Skinnarland aka Einar Hansson
HS 9/1395/3 Maurice Southgate
HS 9/1406/3 Odd Starheim
HS 9/1651 Benjamin Cowburn
TNA HQ 64, MI(R), Functions and Organisation)
WO 373/94 Peter Deinboll
WO 373/108 Gunnar Sønsteby
WO 373/108 Max Manus
WO 373/108 Odd Starheim
WO 373/184 Odd Starheim
Documents in the Imperial War Museum
10057 Sue Ryder, 15 November 1987
13064 Rée, Harry
14093 Private papers, J. McCaffery OBE
29163 John Charrot, 26 June 2006
8688/2 Harry Rée, 1983
8720/3 Harry Rée, 18 January 1985
MH24439
MGH 4324 Cecil Vandepeer Clarke 1942, Special Operations Executive Testing
of Explosive and Incendiary Devices for Sabotage
MGH 4325 Special Operations Executive Testing of Explosive and Incendiary
Devices for Sabotage

Newspapers and Journals

The Belfast Telegraph, 'German U-boats refuelling in Ireland? Surely not', 19
September 2011.
Bergens Tidende, 'First Sabotage Action During the War' (3 September 2001).
The Daily Telegraph, Maurice Buckmaster's obituary, died 17 April 1992.
The Daily Telegraph, 'MI6: The History of the Secret Intelligence Service 1909–
1949 by Keith Jeffery': review by Peter Hennesey, 24 September 2010.
Hertfordshire Countryside, September 1988 (Vol. 43 part 353 pages 30/31):
Story of Brickendonbury: The Home of a Lord Mayor of London, a Chairman
of the East India Company, an Underground Railway Builder, the Special
Operations Executive and now the Malaysian Rubber Producers.
Herts and Essex Observer, 16 Mar 1978 p. 41: Wartime Secret Agents Learned
Their Sabotage Tricks at Brickendonbury.
Herts Mercury, 4 January 1946 p. 5: W.A.E.C. Headquarters : Brickendonbury
Returned to Owner after Being Used by Hertfordshire War Agricultural
Committee.
Herts Mercury, 24 February 1978 p. 61: Wartime Secret Agents Learned Their
Sabotage Tricks at Brickendonbury.
Herts Past & Present, Autumn 2006 (Vol. 3 part 8 pages 3–7): Special Operations
Executive (SOE) in Hertfordshire 1940–1946.
London Gazette, 18 May 1943.
The Times, Birger Stromsheim's obituary, 20 November 2012.

Websites

http://cyberboris.files.wordpress.com/2010/05/kim-philby.jpg
http://elvirabarney.files.wordpress.com/2011/10/michael-stephen.jpg
http://en.wikipedia.org/wiki/MD1
http://en.wikipedia.org/wiki/PIAT
http://en.wikipedia.org/wiki/Thamshavnbanen_sabotage
http://nuav.rforum.biz/t75-aksjonen-mot-bjolvefossen
http://thebravestcanadian.wordpress.com/category/frederic-thornton-peters/
http://thebravestcanadian.wordpress.com/category/royal-navy/
http://web.mac.com/josephcarter76/iWeb/Websted/Peter%20Deinboll.html
http://web.mac.com/josephcarter76/iWeb/Websted/Peter%20Deinboll.html
http://wn.com/Ragnar_Ulstein
http://www.bbc.co.uk/history/worldwars/wwtwo/the_plotters_01.shtml
http://www.bbc.co.uk/ww2peopleswar/stories/34/a5961134.shtml
http://www.bbc.co.uk/ww2peopleswar/stories/51/a5961251.shtml
http://www.belfasttelegraph.co.uk/opinion/columnists/robert-fisk/german-uboats-
    refuelled-in-ireland-surely-not-16051530.html
http://www.brickendonbury.co.uk/pages/Our%20Great%20Estate.pdf
http://www.camp-x.com/officers1942.htm
http://www.compassion-in-business.co.uk/brickendon/brick.php
http://www.cqbservices.com/?page_id=61/
http://www.encyclopedia.com/doc/1O129-plasticexplosives.html http://www.
    encyclopedia.com/topic/SOE.aspx
http://www.holocaustresearchproject.org/nazioccupation/ heydrichkilling.html
http://www.navalandmilitarymuseum.org/resource_pages/heroes/peters.html
http://www.nigelperrin.com/mauricesouthgate.htm
http://www.nrk.no/nyheter/distrikt/nrk_sogn_og_fjordane/fylkesleksikon/853729.
    html
http://www.pbs.org/wgbh/nova/hydro/resistance.html, 'Hitler's Sunken Secret',
http://www.pogledi.rs/diskusije/viewtopic.php?t=2202&sid=6248681d636b07009
    72a30246d29464a
http://www.realmilitaryflix.com/public/253.cfm
http://www.sfclub.org/
http://www.telegraph.co.uk/news/7664351/A-new-mission-for-the-hero-of-
    Telemark.html
http://www.wwiinorge.com/Erik_GjemsOnstad_norg.htm
https://www.cia.gov/news-information/featured-story-archive/office-of-strategic-
    services-training.html
https://www.sis.gov.uk/our-history/buildings.html
www.ww2talk.com/forum/special-forces/29127-telemark-sabotage-battle-heavy-
    water.html

Index